THE LIFE CYCLE LIBRARY

for Young People

The Life Cycle Library

for Young People

REVISED AND UPDATED EDITION

Book
4

GLOSSARY and INDEX

Published by
PARENT AND CHILD BOOKS

REVISED AND UPDATED EDITION
Edited by **Genevieve Millet Landau,** Vice President, Director of Educational Programs and Special Consultant on Child Development at Hasbro Industries, Inc. Formerly Editor-in-Chief, *Parent's Magazine*.

Revised and Updated Edition © 1978 by Parent and Child Books
First Edition © 1969 by Parent and Child Institute

Revised and Updated Edition,
Third Printing, 1979

Brief quotations may be used in critical articles and reviews. For any other reproduction of the book, however, including electronic, mechanical, photocopying, recording or other means, written permission must be obtained from the publisher.

Library of Congress Catalog Card Number: 70-90267

Manufactured in the United States of America

GLOSSARY

abdomen The abdomen is that part of the body below the front of the chest, going down between the hips to the pelvis. The abdomen is sometimes called the belly. The stomach, intestines, and other organs, including the ovaries and uterus in the female, are in the abdominal part of the body.

abnormal Abnormal means different from that which is expected, common, or accepted. It is the opposite of normal.

For example, there are many deviations in growth that are abnormal. A five-year-old boy who is not yet 28 inches tall has an abnormal growth rate. A nine-year-old girl who is more than five feet tall is abnormally tall for her age.

See also: **deviation**

abortion Abortion means "the act of stopping." Specifically, abortion means the act of stopping a pregnancy.

There are two kinds of abortions. One kind is a natural stopping of pregnancy, called a *spontaneous abortion* or *miscarriage*. For many reasons natural forces may end a pregnancy before the normal nine months—usually at some time before the fourth month. In such a case, the embryo comes loose from the wall of the uterus and is passed out of the mother's body.

The second kind of abortion is not the result of natural forces, but is performed as medical treatment. A physician removes the embryo from the mother's uterus in a legal operation performed in a clinic or hospital.

acne Acne is a disease of the skin found most often in adolescents. When puberty begins, certain glands become very active. Among these are the sebaceous glands, which produce fatty material or oil called *sebum*. Too much sebum can cause a clogging of the pores on the surface of the skin. The oil in the clogged pores hardens on exposure to the air, forming blackheads. Often blackheads get mixed with dirt. If blackheads become infected, they get filled with pus and turn into pimples. Pimples usually appear on the face but also often on the neck, back, and shoulders.

Many cures for acne are advertised. Some work and some do not. Any teenager with a bad case of acne should see a doctor. The doctor may use a treatment applied directly to the surface of the skin, or he may prescribe small doses of antibiotics or other drugs. He may also inject various hormones to control the overactive glands.

Proper hygiene helps in the treatment of acne. Pimples should never be squeezed. The face should be washed gently at least three times a day with warm water and soap, preferably germicidal soap. The hair should also be kept clean because oil and dandruff may promote acne. Plenty of sleep and time spent outdoors exercising in the sun can also be helpful. Since too much oil causes acne, oily foods, which may stimulate the sebaceous glands, should be avoided. Some oily foods are chocolate, nuts, peanut butter, fried food, and sharp cheeses. Good foods to eat are those non-oily foods with protein, vitamins, and minerals.

See also: **dermatologist, oil glands**

acquired characteristics Acquired characteristics are those traits that are picked up or learned throughout life. They are different from inherited characteristics which are determined by the chromosomes one gets from his parents.

Some examples of acquired characteristics are mannerisms, ways of speaking, emotional attitude, skills, and sense of humor.

Many different things affect what characteristics a person acquires. The way one is reared by his parents, the places where he lives, and the people he knows help form his character.

See also: **inherited characteristics**

adolescence Adolescence means "becoming adult." Because different people mature at different rates and at different times, it is impossible to set down specific ages as the beginning and end of adolescence. Generally speaking, adolescence begins with the onset of puberty and lasts until the end of the growth period — from about the twelfth year of life to about the twentieth.

During these teenage years a person attains the height, weight, and general body structure that make him physically an adult.

See also: **adult, puberty;** Book 1, Chapter 3, *A Boy Becomes a Man;* Book 1, Chapter 4, *A Girl Becomes a Woman*

adoption Adoption is the act of taking as one's own. Children are usually adopted from child welfare agencies. These agencies care for children when their parents have died or have given them up for adoption shortly after birth. The welfare agencies are run by people who have been trained in the procedures of adoption. Before a couple can adopt a child from one of these agencies, the future parents are carefully interviewed. These agencies also make sure that the adoption is carried out according to the state's adoption laws. A child can also be legally adopted by a stepparent.

adrenal glands The adrenal glands are two endocrine glands which are found in front of and above each kidney. These glands, which produce many hormones, are triangular in shape and have two parts: the adrenal cortex and the adrenal medulla.

The adrenal cortex produces three types of hormones. One group influences carbohydrate, protein, and fat metabolism. Metabolism is the process by which the body uses food and turns it into energy. Another group of hormones produced by the adrenal cortex affects the balance of salt and water in the body. The third group is made up of androgens. Androgens are sex hormones that influence masculine characteristics.

See also: **androgens, endocrine glands, estrogens, hormones, sex hormones**

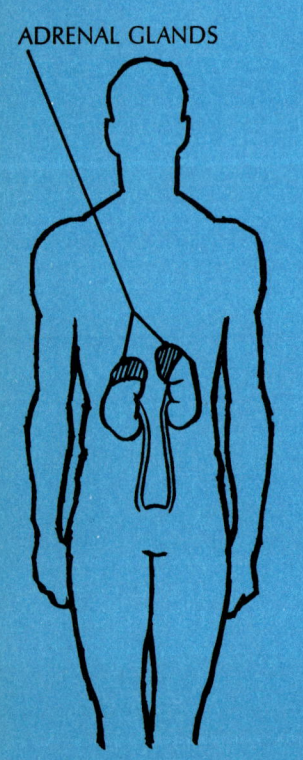

ADRENAL GLANDS

adult Adult means grown-up or mature. An adult is a grown-up person. As an adolescent matures, he finds himself becoming more and more of an adult, both physically and emotionally. His body starts developing adult characteristics, and he learns how to deal with life in an adult manner.

Most states have laws that define the age of an adult. Generally a person is legally considered an adult at the age of 21. In some cases where men are not legally adult until 21, women are of legal adult age at 18.

Reaching a legal adult age means that a person becomes a full citizen and a responsible member of society. If a person abuses his adult privileges, he is responsible for his actions. For example, if an adult breaks a law, he is subject to trial and punishment by his government.

See also: **adolescence, maturation;** Book 1, Chapter 3, *A Boy Becomes a Man;* Book 1, Chapter 5, *A Girl Becomes a Woman*

adultery Adultery is voluntary sexual intercourse between a married person and someone other than his or her own spouse. A married man is committing adultery if he has sexual intercourse with a woman who is not his wife. A married woman is committing adultery if she has sexual intercourse with a man who is not her husband. Sexual intercourse between two consenting unmarried people is legally called fornication.

Adultery is considered a crime in many, but not all, cultures. In our society adultery is punishable by law. In all states it can be grounds for divorce.

Most formal religions forbid adultery. An example of this is found in one of the Ten Commandments from the Bible: "Thou shalt not commit adultery."

afterbirth, see **labor, placenta**

alcohol, see **drinking**

alimony, see **divorce**

amenorrhea, see **menstruation**

amnion The amnion is a thin membrane in the shape of a closed sac that surrounds a developing baby in its mother's uterus.

The amnion is filled with a watery, salt solution called amniotic fluid. The baby, along with the umbilical cord, floats in this fluid and is free to turn, twist, and bounce. The baby is virtually weightless in the amniotic sac.

The amniotic fluid also acts as a shock absorber to protect the baby if his mother falls or is jolted.

Although the baby "swims" as one does in a swimming pool or ocean, he never has to "come up for air." The baby does not drown in the fluid because he does not breathe through his lungs. Instead, he gets oxygen from his mother's blood through the placenta and umbilical cord.

AMNION

The tough, elastic membrane of the amnion stretches as the baby grows, like a balloon that is filled with air. The increasing size of the baby gradually displaces much of the fluid in the amniotic sac. When the baby is ready to be born, the uterus begins to push against the amnion.

Eventually the sac breaks, and it is said that the mother's "bag of waters" has broken. The amniotic fluid flows out of the mother's body, and soon afterward, the baby is born. The tissues and membranes of the amnion are expelled from the mother's body in the afterbirth, along with the placenta and umbilical cord.

See also: **labor, placenta, uterus, vernix**; Book 2, Chapter 9, *How A Baby Develops*

amphetamines, see **drugs**

androgens Androgens is the name given to the entire group of male sex hormones. Androgen is the opposite of estrogen, the name of the female sex hormone group.

Androgens and estrogens are both present in the male and female. Androgens are produced by the testes of men and the ovaries of women. Some androgens are produced by the adrenal glands of both men and women.

The most important job of the androgenic hormones is to cause sexual growth in adolescent boys. Around the time of puberty a boy's body steps up its production of androgens. Androgens circulate through a boy's bloodstream and quicken the growth of his male secondary sex characteristics. Some of these characteristics are facial and pubic hair, lowered voice pitch, and maturing of the testes. The most important androgen, *testosterone*, causes the male sperm to develop.

The role played by androgens in girls is not clearly understood. Most experts agree that androgens are partly responsible for girls' adolescent growth, including sexual development.

See also: **estrogens, secondary sex characteristics, sex hormones, sperm, testicles**

annulment An annulment is a legal act which declares that a marriage never legally existed and is not valid. The word *annul* comes from Latin words which mean "not any." Annulment is different from divorce in that a divorce does not declare that a marriage never legally existed but simply ends a marriage.

The basis of an annulment is the fact that an illegal condition against marriage existed at the time of the marriage. For example, a man may be married to one woman and decide he wants to marry another. If he marries the second woman without telling her about his other wife, he has committed bigamy. If the new wife learns of her husband's other marriage, she may want her own marriage to him dissolved. In this case she can seek an annulment.

See also: **consummation, divorce**

anus The anus is the opening in the rectum for the expulsion of the feces (solid waste) from the body. *Anal* means "pertaining to the anus."

aphrodisiac The word *aphrodisiac* comes from Aphrodite, the ancient Greek goddess of love and beauty. An aphrodisiac is anything that supposedly stimulates sexual desire.

No drugs have been found that actually stimulate a person sexually. Certain substances, such as cantharides, irritate the genital area, but such drugs have no effect on emotional sexual desire.

There are no foods that cause or increase sexual desire or ability. In the past people sometimes ate foods which they thought resembled sex organs in the belief that this would increase their sexual capacities.

Erotic literature, art, and even perfumes may all be called aphrodisiacs if they increase sexual de-

sire. Such things occasionally whet a person's emotional appetite, but they have no physical effect.

artificial insemination Artificial insemination is the artificial placing of semen (containing the sperm cells) in the vagina. Sperm is naturally released in the vagina during sexual intercourse.

When a couple finds that they cannot conceive a child, they sometimes try artificial insemination. The sperm of the husband or another male is placed in the woman's vagina, close to her uterus, by means of a syringe. Artificial insemination is always performed by a doctor. It is hoped that the sperm will join with an egg and cause the woman to become pregnant.

Artificial insemination is often used in animal breeding. It permits animal breeders to breed two animals that live far apart. The semen of the male animal is brought to the female and injected by a veterinarian or by the farmer.

See also: **fertilization, sexual intercourse**

asexual Asexual means without sex. Asexual reproduction is one of the two ways that living creatures produce offspring.

In asexual reproduction the offspring come from one single parent. In sexual reproduction there must be a union of male and female sex cells.

There are three kinds of asexual reproduction. In *division* the parent organism merely splits into two new, equal parts. Each new offspring is a copy of the parent. Amoebas, bacteria, and certain kinds of worms reproduce by division.

Other organisms reproduce by *forming buds*. The parent organism develops a bulge, or bud, on some part of its body. This bud slowly grows into a complete new organism. This new bud either remains attached to its parent, or separates and lives on its own. Sponges and yeast plants form buds to produce offspring.

The third kind of asexual reproduction is that

involving *spores*. The parent organism grows a small, dotlike spore. When the spore becomes ripe, it falls off from its parent. It usually lands on moist ground where it grows into a new organism. Reproduction through spores is found in some forms of plant life such as ferns.

Some organisms, such as jellyfish and corals, can reproduce both sexually and asexually.

See also: **fertilization, reproduction**

athletic supporter, see **jockstrap**

barbiturates, see **drugs**

bastard, see **illegitimate child**

belly button, see **navel**

bigamy, see **monogamy**

birth Birth is the process of being born or coming to life. After fertilization of a mother's egg by a father's sperm, a child grows inside the mother's body. At birth the baby leaves its mother's body, and starts living on its own. Other words for the birth process are *delivery* and *parturition*.

See also: **labor;** Book 2, Chapter 11, *How A Baby Is Born*

birth canal, see **vagina**

birth certificate A birth certificate is an official record of a person's birth. When a child is born, his birth must be reported to the local government. The facts of the child's birth are entered in the government's permanent records, and a birth certificate is given to his parents.

See also: Book 2, Chapter 12, *What Happens to a Newborn*

birth control, see **contraception, family planning**

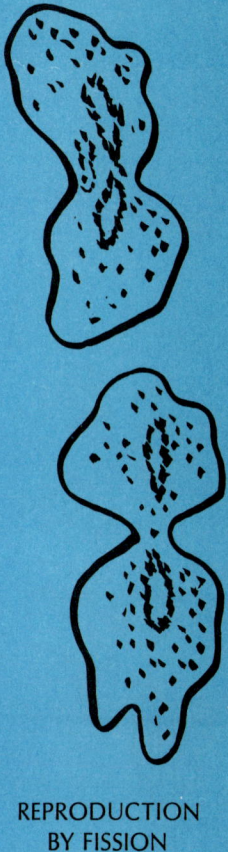

REPRODUCTION BY FISSION

B

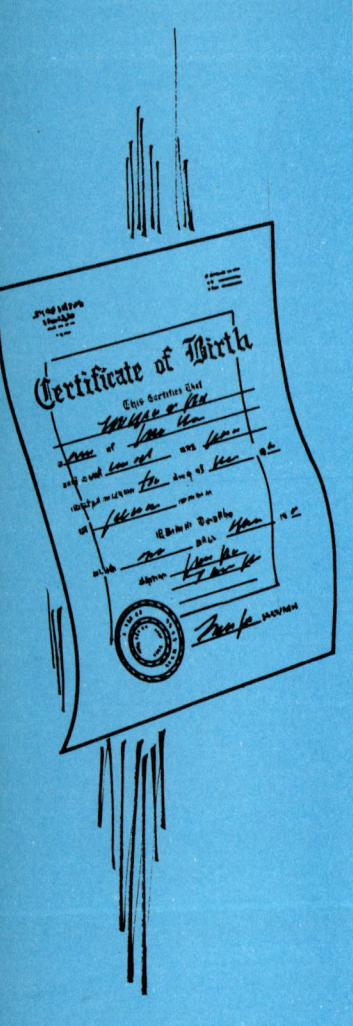

birth defect A birth defect is a physical or mental disorder some babies have when they are born. A birth defect develops sometime during fertilization or embryonic growth. Any mark or damage a baby may receive while he is being born is not technically called a birth defect but a birth injury. Although there are over one thousand kinds of birth defects, they are all very rare. Almost all babies are born healthy and normal.

Birth defects can be caused by the baby's having imperfect genes or by an imbalance in its cells' chromosomes. An error in genes or chromosomes can "show itself" at almost any time during embryonic growth. When the genetic pattern is weak or faulty, the development of any tissue, organ, or bodily function can be affected.

If an embryo is very defective, it has little chance to grow to full term. Nature sometimes stops the growth of a deformed baby. The defective embryo is often naturally aborted early in pregnancy. This occurrence is known as a miscarriage. Not all miscarriages are due to this cause.

There are many new ways to prevent, cure, and treat birth defects. Some defects, such as improper bone growth, may be corrected by surgery. Some defects can be treated by proper diet. There are many organizations that devote all their efforts to finding ways to stop birth defects.

birthmark A birthmark is a blemish or mark on the body of a newborn baby. It is usually brown, red, or purplish. Birthmarks are never caused by the thoughts or feelings of a mother while her baby is growing inside her. The marks are often caused by the way the skin tissues of the baby develop. Birthmarks due to developmental causes are usually permanent. When a baby's birth is helped along with forceps, the pressure of the forceps sometimes leaves marks on the baby's head. Such marks soon disappear.

bisexual Bisexual means of or about both sexes. The term *bisexual* is most often used to describe a person who is sexually interested in both men and women. In biology the term *bisexual* sometimes refers to a person who has both male and female physical characteristics.

As a child grows up, he or she becomes more and more interested in members of the opposite sex. A mature adult who is sexually attracted to both men and women is considered abnormal. Adult bisexuality is considered a sexual deviation by most people.

See also: **hermaphrodite, heterosexuality, homosexuality, lesbianism**

bosom, see **breasts**

bottle baby, see **breast feeding**

brassiere, see **breasts**

breast feeding Breast feeding, or *lactation,* is the process in which a woman feeds a baby by having the infant suck milk from breasts. Of all babies born in recent years in the United States, 25 percent are breast fed. The other 75 percent are bottle fed.

Almost all women are equipped to breast feed (or *nurse*) babies. A woman with small breasts will have just as much food for her baby as a full-bosomed mother. The breasts have tiny *mammary glands* within them that produce milk. A woman's milk passes from these glands through tiny ducts to several small openings in her nipples. When a baby sucks one of her nipples, he gets the milk that her mammary glands have made. Babies naturally know how to suck. Sucking is an instinct that all normal babies have when they are born.

Human milk is good food for a baby. It is always pure, and at the right temperature for the

baby to digest easily. It is filled with all the nutrients and vitamins that a baby needs to grow. A mother's milk also contains special substances that give her baby immunity against infections.

During the first two or three days of his life, a baby gets a special fluid called *colostrum* from his mother's breasts. Colostrum is a watery, yellowish fluid that hardly looks like milk at all. As a baby's sucking on the nipples stimulates his mother's glands, the colostrum will change to milk.

Human milk is slightly bluish in color, and is much thinner than cow's milk. Human milk is just as nutritious as cow's milk, and is made for human babies just as cow's milk is made for calves.

A mother can continue to breast feed her baby as long as she has milk in her breasts, or until she does not want to nurse him any longer. Some women stop breast feeding a few weeks after birth. Other women continue to nurse for six months, and sometimes even for a year or more.

When a woman stops breast feeding, she is said to be *weaning* her child. By the time a baby is weaned, usually his mother has been feeding him solid foods in addition to breast milk for quite a while. Very often a mother will wean her baby when he starts to grow teeth. A baby's teeth, which normally start to grow when he is about six or seven months old, can make breast feeding unconfortable for the mother. Once a woman weans her child and her breasts are no longer stimulated by his sucking, they will stop producing milk.

Breast feeding is the natural way of feeding a new baby. However, bottle-fed babies are just as strong and healthy as breast-fed babies.

See also: **breasts;** Book 2, Chapter 12, *What Happens to a Newborn.*

breast knots Breast knots are small bumps that may appear on a boy's breasts during adolescence. Sometime around puberty a boy's breasts may become sensitive and swollen, and there are knots under the nipples. Breast knots are normal, and are caused by the increased activity of the endocrine glands during adolescence. Breast knots are temporary; they go away within a few weeks or months.

breasts The breasts are the two projecting, milk-producing organs on the chest of a woman. Other names for the breasts are *bosom* and *bust*. In men, the breasts are flat and have no anatomic function. A few years before puberty a girl's breasts start to grow. This is one of the first signs that she is becoming a woman.

The growth of the breasts is stimulated by the female sex hormone, *estrogen*. Usually each nipple grows outward, and the dark circle around the nipple, the *areola,* puffs up. Soon the whole breast begins to expand and gradually fill out.

A girl's breasts may grow unevenly at first. One may start to grow before the other, and for a while they may be different in size. However, their size will become similar once the girl is fully grown. It is not at all unusual, however, for a woman's breasts to be slightly dissimilar in size or shape.

The breasts actually have no muscles of their own, and may sag as they get bigger. Most girls and women wear brassieres (bras) to support their breasts.

When a woman becomes pregnant, her breasts prepare to make milk for her baby. Inside the breasts are tiny glands, called *mammary glands,* surrounded by connective tissue and fat. These glands grow bigger when they are stimulated by hormones during pregnancy. The cells of the glands change into secreting cells. When a woman gives birth to a baby, the milk is made in the glands and passes through ducts to the woman's nipples. A newborn baby drinks his mother's milk by sucking her nipples.

See also: **breast feeding;** Book 1, Chapter 4, *A Girl Becomes a Woman*

breech birth A breech birth is a form of delivery in which the baby is born feet first or buttocks first, instead of head first. About one out of every ten babies enters the world in the breech position.
See also: **birth, labor**

buttocks Buttocks are the two fleshy parts of the body located behind the hips at the lower end of the back. They are the part of the body on which a person sits. The buttocks are sometimes called the *rear end* or the *rump*.

Caesarean birth A Caesarean birth, or Caesarean section, is a surgical way to deliver a baby. For some reason a mother may not be able to give birth to a baby through the birth canal. In such a case, the doctor makes a cut in the wall of her abdomen and uterus. He lifts the new baby out of the mother through this opening. Then he stitches the cut closed, and it soon heals.

This way of being born gets its name from the Caesar family of the Roman Empire. It was during their reign that a law was passed which would permit this operation to be performed only when the mother was very near death. At that time there was no reliable anesthesia or antiseptic surgery, and such an operation was quite dangerous. Some legends say that Julius Caesar himself was born this way. However, this is highly unlikely since his mother survived childbirth and lived to old age.

Today, this way of having a baby is a routine and safe procedure. Only very rarely does a woman suffer any ill effects from it.
See also: **birth, labor**

castration Castration is the removal of the gonads (sex glands). In castration the male's testicles or the female's ovaries are surgically removed.

The testicles and ovaries are the main sources for the sex hormones. After castration, the amount of sex hormones in the body is greatly reduced.

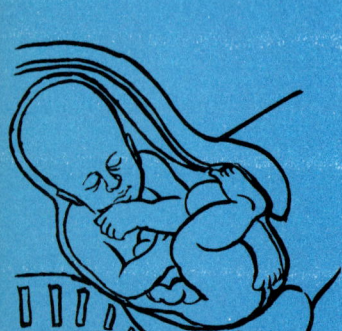
BREECH BIRTH

C

Since the sex glands produce the reproductive cells, castration causes sterility.

A male who has been castrated cannot father a child. A female who has been castrated cannot bear a child. If castration takes place before puberty, no secondary sex characteristics develop.

Castration of male horses is called *gelding*. Gelding makes male horses calmer and more gentle. Female dogs are often castrated in an operation called *spaying* (it is *not* spading).

See also: **ovaries, sex hormones, testicles**

celibacy Celibacy is a term referring to the state of being unmarried. However, celibacy most often means that state of having no sexual intercourse.

A person who never has sexual intercourse is said to be *celibate*. Many people in certain religious groups are celibate. For instance, all nuns and priests of the Roman Catholic Church take vows of celibacy.

cell A cell is the *basic unit of life*. Every living thing is made up of one or more cells. The name *cell* comes from a Latin word meaning "room."

A cell may be almost any shape — round or square or oval, and with regular or irregular outlines — but it is always composed of three parts. These are the *outer wall* or membrane, which surrounds a semi-liquid substance called *cytoplasm*. Inside the cytoplasm is a thicker body called the *nucleus*. The cytoplasm sustains the life activities of the cell; the nucleus contains the hereditary material.

Every living organism grows and continues to exist through cell division, or mitosis.

See also: **meiosis, mitosis, ovum, sperm**; Book 1, Chapter 1, *The Life Cycle*; Book 2, Chapter 13, *Who Will the Baby Be Like*

cervix, see **uterus**

change of life, see **menopause**

SKIN CELLS

BRAIN CELL

character Character refers to all of the moral and ethical traits by which an individual is judged. He may be said to have a strong or weak character. Generally, a person with a strong character stands up for what he believes. A person with a weak character is more likely to yield to pressure. He does not have the strength to live by and defend his ideals. Character is not inherited; it is shaped by such things as desires, experience, knowledge, environment, and ideals. All these qualities make up an individual with a distinct character.

See also: Book 1, Chapter 7, *You Are an Individual*

chastity Chastity is abstention from or avoidance of all sexual activity. In some cases chastity can mean abstention from all "unlawful" sexual activity — usually sex outside of marriage.

Societies and people differ in their attitudes about sexual activity. The usual attitude is to expect that unmarried men and women be chaste, that is, refrain from having intercourse.

See also: Book 3, Chapter 20, *Necking, Petting, and Sexual Feelings*

childbirth, see **birth, labor, natural childbirth**

chromosome A chromosome is one of several threadlike bodies found in the nucleus of all living cells. Each chromosome is made up of many *genes*, the tiny chemical substances which determine hereditary characteristics. Genes are arranged in chromosomes like beads on a necklace.

Each form of life has a special number of chromosomes in each of its cells. For example, white rats have 42, pea plants have 14, and human beings have 46. The only exception to this rule is that mature reproductive cells contain only half the number of chromosomes of that kind of plant or animal. When reproductive cells of each sex combine, they form the total number for that species, and a new individual is begun.

See also: **gene, heredity, mitosis, meiosis;** Book 2, Chapter 9, *How a Baby Develops;* Book 2, Chapter 13, *Who Will the Baby Be Like*

cigarettes, see **smoking**

circumcision Circumcision is the removal of the foreskin from the penis. When a baby is born, the end of his penis is covered with a layer of skin (the foreskin) which can be pushed back away from the end of the penis. Very often the foreskin is cut off, or circumcised, by the doctor shortly after birth. Circumcision is practiced as a religious ritual by the Jews, Moslems, and some other groups.

See also: **foreskin, penis;** Book 2, Chapter 12, *What Happens to a Newborn*

climacteric, see **menopause**

climax, see **orgasm**

clitoris The clitoris is a small female sex organ, highly sensitive to stimulation, composed of tissue similar to that of the male penis. It is called *clitoris*, from the Greek word meaning "to close," because it is partially covered by the labia minora.

The clitoris is cylindrical, and is usually a little less than an inch long. Most of the clitoris is internal, but the tip of it, called the *glans clitoridis*, is on the external part of the body in front of the urethra opening of the genital area. Internally the clitoris consists of spongy tissue filled with many tiny spaces. During sexual excitement, these spaces become filled with blood, causing the clitoris to become erect and enlarged.

See also: **labia, vulva**

coitus, see **sexual intercourse**

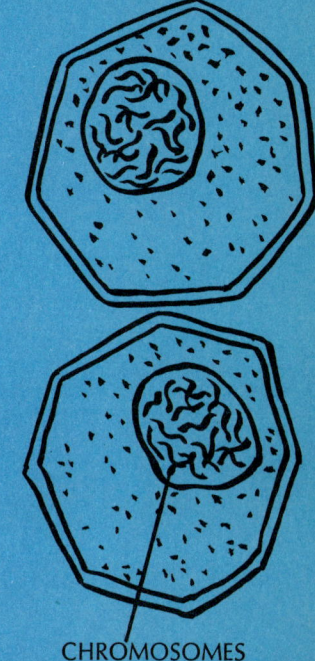

CHROMOSOMES

colostrum, see **breast feeding**

conceive To conceive is to begin the life of a new child. When a man and a woman have sexual intercourse and the woman conceives, they have created a new life. The man's sperm fertilizes the female's egg, and the woman becomes pregnant with their new child. *Conception* is the time at which life is conceived — the time of the union between the sperm and the egg.

See also: **fertilization, sexual intercourse;** Book 2, Chapter 8, *The Beginning of a Life Cycle;* Book 2, Chapter 9, *How a Baby Develops*

condom, see **contraception, prophylactic**

congenital Congenital means present at birth. A baby's congenital traits or defects are formed during his development in the uterus. The word *congenital* does not apply to any characteristics which develop during the birth process itself or after the baby is born.

See also: **birth defect, heredity**

consummation To consummate means to achieve completion or to make perfect. With reference to marriage, consummation means to complete the marriage by having sexual intercourse. If a man and a woman were married but had never had sexual intercourse with each other, the marriage would be unconsummated. The fact that a marriage has not been consummated is grounds for annulment.

See also: **marriage**

contraception Contraception is a general word for any act, method, chemical, or device that prevents conception. When a man and a woman join in sexual intercourse, they may be creating a new life. Contraception is any way they may choose to avoid the possibility of the creation of a new life.

On a large scale, contraception, or birth control, is the means of controlling the world's rapidly growing population. On a small scale, contraception is the way a man and woman can plan their family, and limit their number of children.

The most foolproof method of contraception is *abstinence*. When a man and woman practice abstinence, they do not have sexual intercourse. When they do not have intercourse, there is no opportunity for a sperm to fertilize an egg.

One means of contraception based on abstinence is the *rhythm method*. This is the only form of contraception approved by the Roman Catholic Church. When two people use the rhythm method, they abstain from sexual intercourse around the time of the woman's ovulation. This method is not always reliable because it is difficult for some women to know exactly when they ovulate.

Another method of contraception is *withdrawal*. When a man and a woman are having sexual intercourse, the man must withdraw his penis from the woman's vagina before he ejaculates. This method is seldom effective because it is usually difficult for a man to exercise control when he is sexually excited.

There are many devices a man or woman can use to prevent conception. A man can wear a *condom* on his penis during sexual intercourse. A condom is a rubber device like the finger of a glove. (It is often called a "rubber.") When a man ejaculates, the condom catches his sperm, and prevents it from flowing into the woman's vagina. A condom is not a safe contraceptive method if it breaks or slips off.

A woman can use one of several devices to block sperm from flowing into her uterus. One such device is a *diaphragm*, which a woman inserts into her vagina before intercourse. A diaphragm is a rubber cap that fits over the cervix.

When certain chemicals are placed in the vagina, they block the flow of sperm into the uterus.

These chemicals come in the form of tablets, foams, creams, and jellies.

Two widely used methods of contraception are *oral contraceptives* or the birth control pill (often called simply "the pill") and the *intrauterine device (IUD)*. When a woman swallows birth control pills for a certain number of days (usually 20), she will not ovulate. These pills contain artificial hormones which stop her ovaries from releasing eggs, thus no egg will be present to be fertilized. Only a doctor can prescribe birth control pills. When the pill is used correctly, it is very effective. However, long-term use of the pill is associated with the onset of conditions hazardous to health, especially among women over thirty-five, and those who smoke. Pill-users should have regular medical check-ups.

The IUD is a device, made of metal or plastic, that a doctor inserts into a woman's uterus. It prevents the successful union of the egg and sperm. The IUD usually works best for women who have already had a child.

The most permanent means of contraception is *sterilization*. Sterilization is a surgical operation in which a person is made incapable of reproduction.

Contraception is a serious matter. All couples should realize that no contraceptive, except abstinence, is 100 percent effective.

See also: **conceive, family planning;** Book 2, Chapter 8, *The Beginning of a Life Cycle;* Book 3, Chapter 23, *What About Marriage*

contraceptive, see **contraception**

coordination Coordination is the smooth working together of parts. Physical coordination is the ability to move different parts of the body in a graceful manner at the same time.

Coordination develops slowly as a person matures. A newborn baby can only roll about and swing his arms and legs in the air. Soon he learns to use his hands and fingers, sit up, crawl, and walk. Coordination continues to develop as adolescence approaches. Since adolescence is a time of rapid growth, it sometimes brings with it clumsiness. It takes an adolescent a while to get used to his increasing size and strength.

A tall, slim adolescent boy may have grown so fast that he seems all arms and legs. He may be awkward until his muscles and nervous system adjust to his new size.

A young girl may become very plump during adolescence. She may lack coordination in her walk and posture, but usually an awkward girl eventually grows into a graceful woman.

Coordination for special skills takes practice. Constant exercise is needed to learn to coordinate the arms, hands, and fingers to play the piano. All sports activities require highly developed coordination.

Some people are naturally better coordinated than others. There are very good dancers, and there are those who stumble around a dance floor.

While some people can hardly stay afloat, others easily learn how to swim.

Most people are naturally coordinated well enough to lead a normal, active life. Only in rare cases of disease or accidental injury to the human nervous system is coordination ever seriously damaged.

See also: Book 1, Chapter 5, *Feeling Well;* Book 1, Chapter 6, *What Is Normal?*

copulation, see **sexual intercourse**

corpus luteum Corpus luteum is the name given to an ovarian follicle after a mature egg has been released from it. This tiny sac produces sex hormones important in the reproductive cycle.

Following ovulation, cells in the empty follicle begin to multiply rapidly to fill the space where the egg was contained. Since these cells are yellow

D

in color, the follicle is then called *corpus luteum*, which means "yellow body" in Latin.

See also: **ovulation**

cramps, see **menstruation**

crush A crush is a feeling of strong infatuation. It is an intense romantic feeling for someone of the same or opposite sex that lasts for a short time.

Almost all young people have crushes at one time or another. A young girl may have a crush on one of her school friends. She may want to spend all of her time with her. Young boys may have crushes on a teacher or camp counselor. The older man may seem like a god, and the young boy worships him as a hero.

Crushes are a normal part of growing up. As teenagers become interested in people of the opposite sex, they often have a number of crushes.

See also: **infatuation, love, romance;** Book 3, Chapter 22, *How Do You Know When It's Love*

custody, see **divorce**

dating Dating is having a social engagement with a person of the opposite sex. In most cases, the time and event of a date are arranged beforehand.

In the United States, where individuals select their own marriage partners, dating is the best way to learn about members of the opposite sex. It is also a good way to have fun. The dating system practiced in this country is considerably different from that practiced in many other countries. For example, in Europe, group dating may begin in high school, but not until later (when the time for marriage is closer), do couples pair off into single dating. In countries where parents still select marital partners for their children, dating, as it is known in the U.S., does not exist.

By the time most boys and girls graduate from high school, they have had some experience in dating. Some adolescents may be more interested in sports, school activities, or hobbies, however, and may not start dating until a much later age. Others may not be relaxed in a dating situation until they are in college.

See also: Book 3, Chapter 18, *Dating for Girls;* Book 3, Chapter 19, *Dating for Boys;* Book 3, Chapter 20, *Necking, Petting, and Sexual Feelings*

defloration Defloration is the stretching or breaking of the hymen that usually occurs during a woman's first sexual intercourse. Sometimes the hymen is surgically ruptured before marriage. Defloration can also occur as a result of athletics or accident.

See also: **hymen, virginity**

delivery, see **labor**

dermatologist A dermatologist is a physician who specializes in the treatment of the skin and its disorders. His main diagnostic tool is observation of the disorder. He also considers bodily measurements, such as metabolic rate and blood count, as well as the patient's personal health history.

A dermatologist is the doctor to consult for help in treating acne and other skin problems that may occur during the years of adolescence.

deviation Deviation means any type of departure from the established pattern. Sexual deviation is a term that has traditionally referred to any sexual activities outside the socially accepted male-female relationship.

diaphragm, see **contraception**

diet Diet includes all of the liquid and solid food a person normally consumes. Since food is the body's key to maintaining proper energy, growth, and function, diet affects physical and mental

health. A good diet does not depend only on *how much* food is eaten, but also on *what kind*. A good diet is a *balanced diet*—one that contains all of the nutrition needed at a particular time.

An adolescent's diet should provide maximum energy and nutrition. During these years of great growth and activity, a recommended daily balanced diet includes: four or more servings of vegetables or fruit; four or more cups of milk or milk products; three or more servings of meat; and four or more servings of bread and/or cereal products.

See also: **nutrition;** Book 1, Chapter 5, *Feeling Well*

divorce Divorce is the legal ending of a marriage. After a divorce, both partners are legally single and are free to marry again. In the United States, each state has its own laws regarding divorce. Actions that may be grounds for divorce in one state may not be in another. The only single reason recognized in all 50 states is adultery.

Religions, too, have regulations regarding divorce. For example, the Roman Catholic Church does not permit or recognize divorce. According to Orthodox and Conservative Jewish law, divorce must be approved by religious authorities as well as civil authorities before either partner can remarry. Reform Judaism accepts civil divorce as sufficient. Protestants recognize civil divorce.

Why do people get divorced? The obvious reason is that they no longer wish to be married to each other. But the reasons for *that* are perhaps as many and varied as the number of divorced people. The serious nature of divorce as a social problem can be realized from the fact that one out of four marriages entered into today may be expected to end in divorce court in the future.

When a husband and wife have no children, their divorce concerns only them, and it is a relatively simple matter. There will be a question of the division of property and of *alimony* (the money a man must pay to his divorced wife unless she gives up her right to it), but that is usually the end of it. When one or more children are involved, many things must be taken into consideration. Who will have custody of the children? Generally, custody is awarded to the mother, and the father is given certain visiting rights. Mutual custody is also a possible arrangement. Who will be responsible for the children's financial support? The law in most states requires a man to support his children whether he is married to their mother or not. The amount of that support is based on his ability to pay.

Even more important than the financial questions are the considerations of how a divorce will affect the children psychologically. Most child study authorities believe that it is better for a child to live with one happy parent than with two miserable ones. There are no easy answers to the question of divorce.

See also: **annulment, marriage;** Book 3, Chapter 23, *What About Marriage*

DNA, see **gene**

dope, see **drugs**

double standard The double standard is an unofficial code of society according to which two different standards are used to evaluate male and female behavior, especially regarding sexual matters. A society that functions according to a double standard permits men much more freedom than it allows women. For example, it may express little or no disapproval of men having premarital or extramarital sexual relations, while severely criticizing women for the same kind of behavior.

See also: **moral**

douche A douche is a washing out of the vagina. This cleansing may be done for sanitary or medical

purposes. Water or some other liquid is used. Most physicians believe that regular douching is not necessary, that the natural substances in the vagina are enough to keep it clean. Too much douching can sometimes destroy these substances.

Douching for the purpose of contraception is useless, because ejaculation will have placed some sperm beyond the reach of a stream of water, even if it used immediately following intercourse.

drinking The term *drinking*, as it is commonly used, means drinking alcoholic beverages such as beer, wine, and whiskey. Throughout recorded history, many different customs and traditions have been associated with drinking. In the United States today, there is no fixed pattern of drinking. Some groups prohibit the consumption of alcohol in any form. Some people may drink only one or two highballs (alcohol mixed with soda or water and served with ice) at parties or with guests in their own home. Others may have cocktails before dinner, beer while watching television, or may drink in nightclubs, taverns, or restaurants.

When a person drinks, the alcohol is quickly absorbed into the blood system. It is carried by the blood to all parts of the body where it causes some or all of the following to happen: It reduces mental abilities, muscle coordination, and balance. It depresses the parts of the mind which control such things as judgment and inhibitions.

If the amount of alcohol increases further, the drinker gradually becomes intoxicated. He is less aware of his environment and less able to control his coordination. He may feel sick, or vomit. Eventually alcohol causes most people to fall asleep. (If too much alcohol is consumed at a particular time, it can depress vital body functions, such as the heart, and can cause death.)

Because of the intoxicating effects of alcohol and the problems that arise if people use it to excess, governments maintain control over it. In this country, the federal and state and local governments have laws dealing with the production, sale, and consumption of alcohol. All states forbid the sale of alcohol to *minors*, people who are legally not of age to drink. In most states the legal age for drinking is 21; in some it is 18.

See also: Book 3, Chapter 21, *Parents Watch the Clock*

drugs Drugs are chemical substances which affect physical and mental functions. They are used legally by physicians to prevent or cure disease, or to improve physical or mental well-being.

The misuse or illegal use of drugs is a major health problem, especially among young people. Taking drugs, or *dope,* is an experiment for some, a social activity for others, and a habit for many.

Four classes of drugs are used illegally: hallucinogens, stimulants, depressants, and narcotics.

Hallucinogens are often called *psychedelics*, which means "mind expanding." They are *not* physically addicting. *Addiction* means dependence on or yielding to the effects of something to such an extent that being deprived of that substance will cause severe physical stress. Hallucinogenic drugs cause people to have hallucinations, that is, to see, feel, smell, or in some way "sense" something that exists only in their mind. The two most commonly used are marijuana and LSD.

Marijuana is also known as *pot, grass, tea, hemp,* and *Mary Jane.* Marijuana cigarettes are called *joints. Hashish* or *hash* is a stronger form of marijuana. Both come from the leaves and flower tops of the Indian hemp plant, *cannabis sativa.* Marijuana can be smoked, eaten, or sniffed. Effects can be felt in a few minutes, last for varying lengths of time, vary considerably for different people at different times, and cannot be predicted. Some people may feel "high" (as in alcohol intoxication), talkative, dreamy, and happy. Others may be confused, quiet, angry, or afraid. Marijuana has

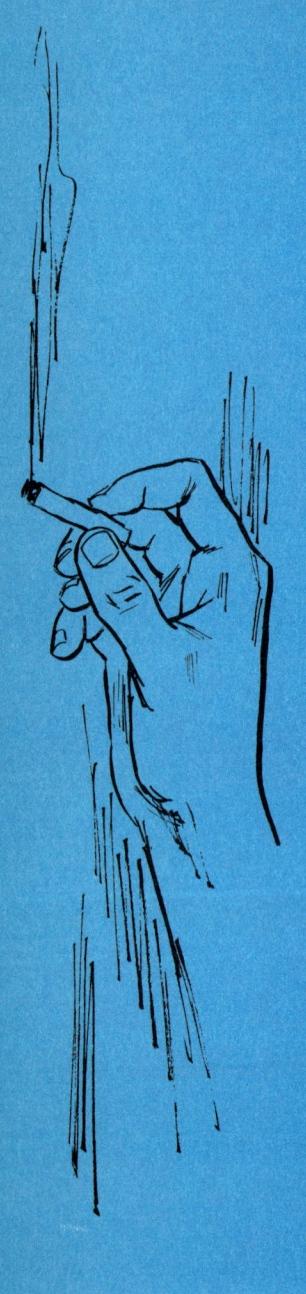

only recently been subjected to scientific study, although the hemp plant has been cultivated for its escape-producing effects for centuries. Marijuana is considered one of the least damaging of all the drugs presently in use.

LSD (lysergic acid diethylamide) is the strongest of all hallucinogens. Among its users it is known as *acid, cubes, trips, heavenly blues, and pearly gates.* LSD is produced synthetically and is taken in capsules, pills, and in a tasteless liquid soaked on sugar cubes or crackers.

Effects of LSD are not yet known with complete accuracy. It does produce extreme fantasies. Users may hear unearthly music, see brilliant colors or strange objects, or believe they are on a "trip" to some magical place. They can be extremely happy or terribly depressed.

LSD is dangerous. It can cause or increase psychotic, suicidal, or homicidal tendencies. The drug may produce changes in the brain that are not evident until weeks or longer after it was taken. Some users have required psychiatric treatment and others have seriously injured or even killed themselves. Scientists are studying the possibility that LSD can also affect chromosomes, causing danger to future offspring of users.

Stimulants are drugs that give the user an emotional lift. Some names for stimulating drugs are *uppers, pep pills, bennies, dexies, footballs, and co-pilots.* One type of stimulant, *amphetamines,* is used legally to inhibit appetite, relieve depression, and produce a "wide awake" feeling. Amphetamines can cause hallucinations or psychoses, high blood pressure, and heart attacks. *Methamphetamine,* also called *speed* and *methedrine,* is extremely dangerous. It literally speeds up all body processes to such an extent that they become "burned out," and the user dies. *Cocaine,* another stimulant, can cause happy or hallucinatory feelings. In an overdose it can cause convulsions or paralyze heart and lungs, causing death.

Effects of all stimulants are excitement, extra energy, hyperactivity, and a feeling that sleep is not necessary. Stimulants can cause psychological dependence. When people stop using such drugs they suffer mental and physical depression.

Depressants are drugs that are used to help relieve nervousness and insomnia (sleeplessness). The main group of depressants are *barbiturates*, known by such names as *downers, goofballs, candy, yellow jackets, rainbows,* and *blue devils.* Many people misuse barbiturates and become dependent upon them to relieve tension, to induce sleep, or to produce "highs."

Effects of depressants are to make people either extremely relaxed, sociable, and happy or, conversely, to make them sluggish, unhappy, or quarrelsome. Dangers from overdose are coma or death from failure of the respiratory system.

Narcotics are drugs that are prescribed legally for relief of pain. Most are habit forming, and addiction to them is a serious social problem.

Opium comes from a type of poppy. It has been used for centuries to relieve pain, and has also been smoked by people to whom it brings escape from life in the form of "opium dreams."

Morphine and *codeine* are derived from opium and have similar effects. Morphine is most commonly obtained in sleeping pills and codeine in cough medicines.

Heroin was first produced synthetically in 1898. Many war-wounded soldiers had become dependent upon morphine and it was thought that heroin would be a good "safe" substitute. Today, heroin is not used legally in the United States. It is completely illegal, and is known to its users as *the big H, horse,* or *junk.* It is either inhaled or injected directly into a vein. It appeals to some people because it makes them "feel good" and inhibits fear and tension, causing a person to forget his problems and responsibilities. The effect of one dose usually lasts only about three hours and,

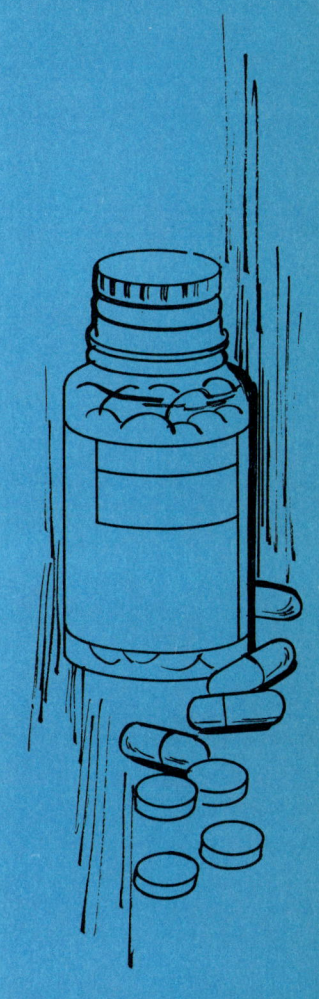

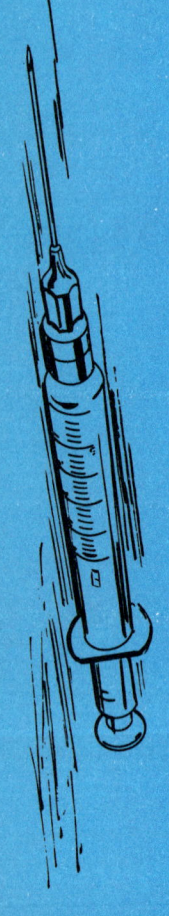

because it is an addictive drug, the user's body craves more heroin. The addict must continue to take heroin or go through a horribly painful period of "withdrawal" from the drug. A person can become addicted to or "hooked on" heroin after only a week of daily use. Addicts find their habit expensive to support, and most find they must turn to crime in order to pay for the drug.

Other harmful substances. Sniffing airplane glue, hair spray, paint thinner, lighter fluid, and other such substances is a fad which some young people seem to think of as an innocent adventure. These things are not drugs, but they can cause similar serious damage and even death. Products used for "sniffing" can be poisonous. They have caused permanent damage to the brain, liver, and nervous system of some and have killed others.

See also: Book 3, Chapter 21, *Parents Watch the Clock*

dysmenorrhea, see **menstruation**

effeminate   The word *effeminate* is used to describe a male who has a number of female characteristics. Some of these characteristics might be lack of strength, soft curves of the body, or a high voice. Some men who are effeminate are homosexuals. A greater number of men with effeminate characteristics lead normal, heterosexual lives.

See also: **homosexuality, masculinity**

egg, see **ovum**

ejaculation   Ejaculation is the discharge of semen from the penis. It occurs at the climax of sexual excitement (orgasm). Ejaculation is a series of short, quick spurts of semen. In an average ejaculation, the milky-white semen measures about a teaspoonful and contains from 200 million to 500 million sperm.

See also: **fertilization, orgasm, penis, sperm**

embryo An embryo is a fertilized human egg in its second stage of growth. During the first stage, from conception to the second week, it is called a *zygote*. From the second to the eighth week it is called an *embryo,* and from the eighth week until birth the developing baby is called a *fetus*.

See also: **fertilization, fetus, zygote;** Book 2, Chapter 9, *How a Baby Develops*

emission, see **seminal emission**

endocrine glands The word *endocrine* means "secreting (producing and giving off) internally." Endocrine glands secrete their substances directly into the bloodstream of animals and humans. Other glands, called *exocrine* glands, secrete their substances externally through ducts or tubes.

The substances that the endocrine glands secrete are called *hormones*. Hormones are chemical messengers that travel in the bloodstream to every part of the body. They influence such things as mental ability, physical activity, hair growth, voice pitch, and sexual behavior.

The four most important endocrine glands are the pituitary, the thyroid, the adrenal glands, and the gonads. These four endocrine glands, with their hormones, affect the activity of every cell.

The *pituitary gland* is located at the base of the brain. It is controlled by a part of the brain called the *hypothalamus*. The pituitary gland secretes hormones which are responsible for the body's growth. It also secretes hormones which affect the other glands. This is why the pituitary is often called the "master" endocrine gland. The *thyroid* is found in the neck. It is responsible for control of the body's metabolism. Metabolism is the way in which food is used and stored by the body's cells.

The *adrenal glands* lie above the kidneys. The adrenals have two parts called the adrenal cortex and the adrenal medulla. One hormone secreted by the adrenal cortex, like the thyroid hormone,

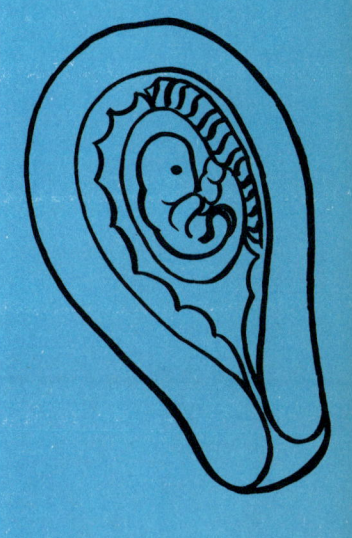

EMBRYO

affects the body's metabolism. Another cortex hormone influences the balance of water and salt in the body. A third hormone plays a part in sexual growth. The adrenal medulla secretes a hormone that helps the body react to stress or emergency situations.

The fourth endocrine glands are the *gonads*. The gonads are the sex glands of the male and female. The male gonads are the testes, and the female, the ovaries. The gonads are directly stimulated by the pituitary hormones. The gonads secrete hormones that promote the growth of the secondary sex characteristics: underarm hair, pubic hair, facial hair in males, and breast development in females. The gonads also produce the male the female reproductive cells, sperm and ovum.

The body's growth, sexual development, and ability to reproduce are controlled by the endocrines. Their hormones maintain the body's delicate chemical balance. The endocrine glands influence the way one feels, thinks, and behaves.

See also: **adrenal glands, exocrine glands, pituitary gland, sex hormones, thyroid gland**

engagement An engagement is a mutual promise of a future marriage. A man and woman who are engaged to each other do not date other people. They set a date for their wedding and announce it to their family and friends. Usually the man gives the woman a ring, called an engagement ring, as a symbol of their coming marriage. There is no set length of time that an engagement lasts.

See also: **dating, marriage;** Book 3, Chapter 23, *What About Marriage*

environment Environment is a general term used to describe all conditions or influences (other than heredity) that affect life. Included in a person's environment are such things as: the type of home, parents, teachers, and friends he has; the school he goes to or the neighborhood he plays in; his exposure to certain hobbies, sports, or beliefs; the food he eats and the diseases he has. (The first nine months of life in the womb are also part of the environment—the pre-natal environment.) All of these, plus many other influences, shape each individual's intelligence, physical appearance, and personality.

See also: **acquired characteristics, heredity, inherited characteristics;** Book 2, Chapter 13, *Who Will the Baby Be Like*

epididymis The epididymis is a mass of tiny tubes attached to the back portion of each testicle in the male. If the epididymis tubes were stretched out end to end, they would be more than 20 feet long. After the sperm cells leave the testicles, they are stored and they mature in the epididymis. A secretion from the epididymis mixes with the sperm before it passes to the vas deferens.

See also: **sperm, testicles, vas deferens**

erection An erection is the penis in a rigid, hard state. A penis becomes erect when blood flows down into the tissues of the organ and fills them. Erection can occur in males of any age, from infants to old men. It is a direct result of sexual stimulation, and sexual intercourse is impossible unless the penis is erect. However, erection can occur, especially in young boys, for many other reasons. Among these are having stimulating dreams, lifting very heavy loads, irritation from tight clothing, or exposure to cold.

See also: **penis, potency, sexual intercourse**

erogenous zones Erogenous means sexually sensitive or stimulating. An erogenous zone is a part or area of the body which is sexually sensitive. Some erogenous zones are the lips, breasts and nipples, buttocks, and external genitals.

erotic Erotic describes that which is related to

sexual love or stimulation. For instance, a love scene in a movie or a beautiful painting of a nude can both be erotic. The word *erotic* is formed from the name of the Greek god of love, Eros.

See also: **aphrodisiac**

estrogens Estrogens are the female sex hormones. They are produced by the ovaries, and serve many purposes. One of their jobs is to prepare young girls for womanhood. Estrogens promote the growth of secondary sex characteristics such as the breasts and pubic hair. During each menstrual cycle they stimulate the pituitary to produce hormones which cause an egg to mature and ovulate.

When a woman is pregnant her estrogens stop stimulating the pituitary and additional eggs are not released. Estrogens used in contraceptive pills "mimic" the hormone balance of pregnancy. This prevents pregnancy by stopping the release of an egg which could be fertilized.

Estrogens also help to prepare the uterus for pregnancy. They thicken the uterine wall and stimulate the growth of small uterine glands. Estrogens also stimulate the mammary (milk-producing) glands in the breasts.

See also: **androgens, breasts, contraception, menstruation, ovaries, secondary sex characteristics**

exhibitionism Exhibitionism is a type of behavior in which a person exposes his genitals.

The exhibition of sexual organs is normal to a certain extent. Sexual intercourse usually involves nudity of the two partners. Small children sometimes openly display their genitals, but this behavior is thought to be normal in small children.

However, public exhibitionism by an adult is considered abnormal. It is a crime in most states and is punishable by law. The criminal exhibitionist is most often a man who exposes his penis in public to female strangers. A public exhibitionist is probably emotionally disturbed. He has little control over his actions, and probably needs psychiatric help. Exhibitionism is one of the most common sexual offenses.

exocrine glands Exocrine glands are glands which pass their secretions to the internal or external body surfaces, such as the lining of the mouth or the skin, through tiny ducts. They differ from the endocrine (ductless) glands which secrete hormones directly into the blood or lymph systems. Some examples of exocrine glands are the *salivary glands* which secrete saliva into the mouth, *sebaceous glands* which secrete oil on the skin, and *sweat glands* which secrete watery fluid through pores of the skin.

See also: **endocrine glands, oil glands**

extramarital, see **adultery, marital**

facts of life The phrase "facts of life" is a popular expression for the explanation of the human reproductive process. This explanation usually concerns information about the genitals, menstruation, sexual intercourse, fertilization, and gestation.

See also: **sex education**

Fallopian tubes The Fallopian tubes are two muscular canals in the female body. Each tube is attached to the uterus at one end, and extends but is not attached to an ovary at the other end. They are sometimes called oviducts or uterine tubes. These tubes were named after the scientist Fallopius, who first described them.

The Fallopian tubes are about five to seven inches long and 1/16 of an inch in diameter. When an ovum (or egg) is released from an ovary, it passes into one of the Fallopian tubes. If a sperm joins with and fertilizes the egg, it usually does so while the egg is still in one of the tubes. The egg, whether fertilized or not, then travels down the tube and into the uterus.

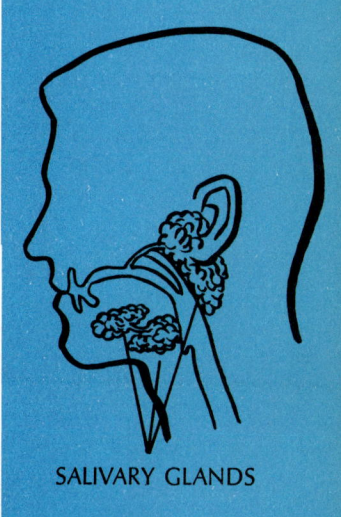

SALIVARY GLANDS

FALLOPIAN TUBES

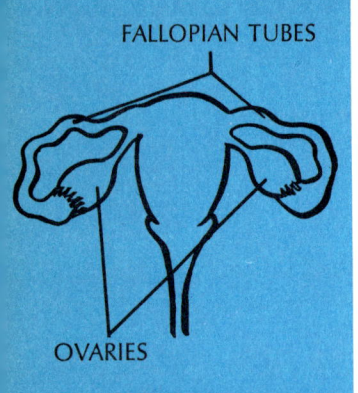

OVARIES

Sometimes the movement of the fertilized egg through the Fallopian tube may be blocked. In this case the egg, or embryo, may attach itself to the wall of the tube and begin to grow. This is technically a pregnancy, and it is called an ectopic, tubal, or extrauterine pregnancy. In almost all cases, the fetus must be surgically removed because it could cause the wall of the tube to rupture.

See also: **ovaries, ovulation, uterus**

family planning When a married couple decide how many children they wish to have and when they wish to have them, they are practicing family planning. Another name for regulating the size of a family is *planned parenthood*. It is now possible to plan the number and spacing of children because the process of conception is understood. Married couples know that conception is most likely to occur during the time of ovulation. They also know that conception can be avoided by the use of a contraceptive device and/or method that prevents the union of egg and sperm during intercourse. Oral contraceptives ("the pill") are also used. Some religious groups feel that family planning is morally improper. Other religious groups feel this is a private matter for each individual to decide according to his conscience.

See also: **conceive, contraception**

feces Feces is solid waste matter. It is formed in the bowel, or intestine, passes to the rectum, and is expelled from the body through the anus in the process of *defecation*.

See also: **urine**

female In all forms of life that continue their species by sexual reproduction, the female is the parent that produces the eggs. This is true of both plants and animals.

In mammals, including human beings, the eggs are fertilized by the male sperm to continue the life cycle. In all but a few rare cases, the female carries the developing offspring in her uterus (womb) until birth, and cares for it thereafter. The female is the mother of the new individual.

The word *female* also refers to all physical organs, traits, and characteristics found only in the female sex. In human beings, these are the things that contribute to femininity.

See also: **femininity**; Book 1, Chapter 4, *A Girl Becomes a Woman;* Book 2, Chapter 10, *The Mother of the Baby*

female reproductive system, see **reproductive organs**

femininity Femininity is the total of those attributes that characterize women rather than men. It is expected that a woman will have a more delicate body build, a softer voice, and less physical strength than a man. Other traits, such as tenderness, gentleness, sympathy, which we usually associate with femininity (as opposed to masculinity) may not be an essential part of womanliness, but qualities encouraged by the culture.

See also: **masculinity, sexuality;** Book 1, Chapter 4, *A Girl Becomes a Woman*

feminism Feminism is the belief in the complete political, economic, and social equality of the sexes. Feminists carry on organized activity to further women's rights and interests. In the United States, they secured for women the right to vote.

fertility Fertility refers to the condition of being able to produce offspring. That depends on many things. A healthy sperm must meet with a healthy egg, and the fertilized egg must be nourished and carried by the woman until birth. If the male or female cannot fully take part in this process, then he or she is not fertile. A living thing that is not fertile is said to be *sterile*.

See also: **fertilization, sterility**

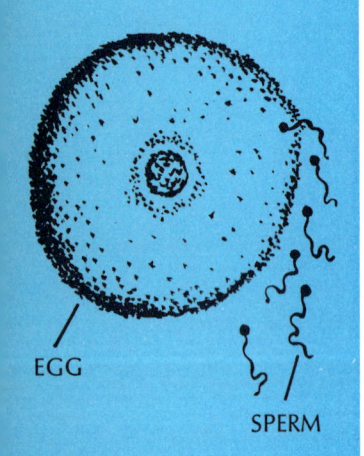

fertilization Fertilization, also called *conception,* is the union of a male sperm with a female ovum, which begins the life of a new individual.

Before fertilization is possible in humans, certain conditions must exist. Both the male and female must be sexually mature individuals who produce healthy, mature reproductive cells. Also, sperm must be present in the Fallopian tube near the time of ovulation, so that both the egg and sperm are alive and active.

When sperm are ejaculated into the vagina during sexual intercourse, they travel through the uterus to the Fallopian tubes. Sperm in the tube where an egg is present are immediately attracted to the egg. (If ovulation has not occurred, sperm are able to survive at least two days while waiting for an egg.)

Of the millions of sperm surrounding the egg, only one is able to fertilize it. It is believed that as this sperm penetrates the outer membrane of the egg cell, the egg gives off a chemical that keeps other sperm from entering. The sperm's tail dissolves, while the head containing the nucleus moves toward the nucleus of the egg. When the 23 chromosomes of the sperm unite with the 23 chromosomes of the egg, fertilization has occurred. Together, they form the 46 chromosomes necessary to begin the life of a new human being.

Following fertilization, the fertilized egg (called a *zygote*) begins to develop by cell division as it moves toward the uterus, where it will grow during pregnancy.

See also: **artificial insemination, conceive, fertility, ovum, sperm;** Book 2, Chapter 9, *How a Baby Develops*

fetus Fetus (also spelled *foetus*) is the term used to describe an unborn human being in its third and final stage of development. From conception to the second week, the developing cell mass is called a *zygote.* From the second week to the eighth, it is called an *embryo*. From the eighth week of development, by which time most of the basic body parts have been formed, it is called a *fetus* until birth.

See also: **embryo, fertilization, zygote;** Book 2, Chapter 9, *How a Baby Develops*

foam, see **contraception**

forceps A forceps is a metal instrument that looks something like tongs. It is used for grasping objects and holding them firmly. A forceps is sometimes used in the delivery of a baby. The doctor puts the forceps into the mother's vagina and grasps the baby, usually by the head. He then gently pulls the baby through the vagina, helping him to be born. Occasionally the tips of the forceps leave tiny marks on the sides of the baby's head. These marks disappear soon after birth.

See also: **labor;** Book 2, Chapter 11, *How a Baby Is Born*

foreskin The foreskin is the loose fold of skin which partly covers the tip, or head (*glans*), of the penis.

Soon after birth, many baby boys are circumcised. Circumcision is the cutting away of the foreskin. Removal of the foreskin makes it easier to keep the penis clean.

When an uncircumcised penis is not erect, the foreskin almost completely covers the tip of the penis. When the penis becomes erect during sexual excitement, the foreskin retracts, or pulls back, and the tip of the penis becomes exposed. Another name for the foreskin is the *prepuce*.

See also: **circumcision, penis**

fornication Fornication is the term applied to sexual intercourse between a man and a woman who are not married to each other.

Determining that an act of intercourse is fornication is primarily a legal distinction. Committing

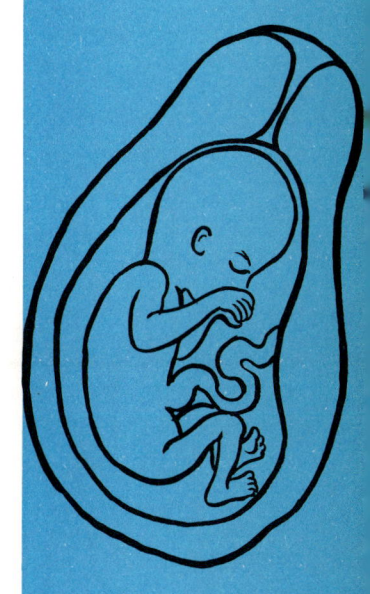

FETUS

an act of fornication is punishable by law in most states, although the laws are seldom enforced.

See also: **adultery**

foster care Foster care is the rearing of children outside of their own homes, either in a foster home or in an institution. This type of care is necessary when a child's own parents are unable or unwilling to care for him, due to a serious illness, economic problem, death, or some other difficulty.

Social agencies exist which look after the welfare of such children. They attempt to place them in foster homes where they are given the personal care, love, and attention found in any good home. Children who are emotionally disturbed, or who would not benefit from the intimacy of a foster family, are usually placed in an institution.

People who wish to be foster parents must have an income adequate to care for their own family. They must be in good physical and mental health, and be able to give the foster child a bed of his own. If they meet these qualifications, they are licensed by the state, and receive payment to help care for foster children they accept.

Foster care differs considerably from adoption, which is a permanent situation. A foster child is often away from his natural parents only temporarily, and returns to them when the family difficulty no longer exists.

See also: **adoption**

fraternal twins, see **multiple birth**

frigidity Frigidity is sexual coldness in women. The term is used most often to describe a woman who cannot feel sexual pleasure.

The basis of frigidity is usually psychological. Some women who are frigid refuse to permit themselves to experience sexual desire. Others may become sexually aroused but be unable to enjoy sexual intercourse or to achieve an orgasm. It is entirely possible for a woman who is frigid to take part in intercourse and to conceive a child.

See also: **orgasm, sex drive, sexual intercourse**

full-term baby A full-term baby is one who is born when the gestation period is completed. The gestation period for human beings is approximately 280 days, or nine months. At the end of nine months the baby is fully prepared to enter the world outside his mother's womb. Infants born before the full term of their mother's pregnancy are called *premature* babies. They are able to survive and function like full-term babies only when given special care.

See also: **premature birth**

gender, see **sex**

gene Genes, tiny chemical substances found in the chromosomes of all cells, are the basic units of heredity. They contain special chemical "messages" that determine the hereditary traits of each living being.

Genes dictate heredity by their principal chemical, *deoxyribonucleic acid* (*DNA*), the basic substance of all life. DNA is made up of substances that can be arranged in an almost infinite number of ways, just as letters of the alphabet can be arranged in different ways for different words. The *specific* way DNA is arranged in genes determines: 1) the distinguishing traits of each species (for example, it determines why dogs are different from cats); and 2) the unique traits of individuals within each species (each human is different from every other human).

There are genes that give the blueprint or message for the development of physical features. Different genes, for example, determine eye color, eye size, and eye shape.

A person's heredity results from the combination of genes from both his mother and father.

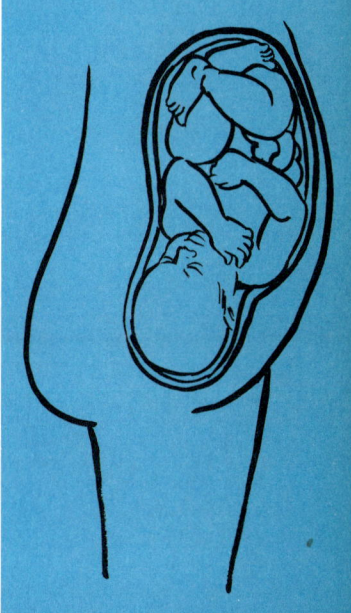

FULL-TERM BABY

G

GENE

CHROMOSOME

410

When the chromosomes of the sperm and egg unite during fertilization, some genes have a stronger influence than others. A *dominant gene* is one that usually dictates a particular characteristic. A *recessive gene* is one that usually does not influence characteristics of the new individual, but which remains hidden in his chromosomes. For example, the gene for black hair is dominant. A corresponding recessive gene is for blond hair. When these two different genes meet during fertilization, the dominant gene will have the stronger influence. The new baby will have black hair. His recessive gene for blond hair will remain hidden in his chromosomes and will appear in some of his reproductive cells when he matures. Recessive genes do influence heredity when both the sperm and the egg carry the same type of recessive gene.

See also: **cell, chromosome, heredity, inherited characteristics, meiosis**; Book 1, Chapter 2, *The Miracle of Growth*; Book 2, Chapter 9, *How a Baby Develops*; Book 2, Chapter 13, *Who Will the Baby Be Like*

generation Generation has three meanings. It comes from the Latin word meaning "to bring into existence," and in that sense refers to the fact of reproduction. It also means a group of individuals all born and living during approximately the same period of time, as in the phrase "the silent generation." Historically, a generation can mean the time span between the birth of parents and the birth of their offspring. From this last meaning comes the expression "the generation gap."

generation gap Generation gap refers to the differences in values between an older and a younger generation—between parents and their children.

Often the generation gap is widest during a child's adolescence. It is during these years that a **young person is most likely to form opinions of his own and to question his parents' values.**

In a broader sense, young people sometimes rebel against what they consider the entire social structure of the older generation. The younger generation often protests against traditions in politics, religion, and morals.

See also: Book 3, Chapter 16, *You and Your Family;* Book 3, Chapter 21, *Parents Watch the Clock*

genetics Genetics is the study of the hereditary traits passed on from parent to offspring. It is a branch of the biological sciences, and deals with plants, animals, and human beings.

See also: **heredity, inherited characteristics;** Book 2, Chapter 13, *Who Will the Baby Be Like*

genitals Genitals is another word for the reproductive organs. It is used especially in reference to the external reproductive organs, such as the penis.

See also: **reproductive organs**

germ cell Germ cell is another name for a reproductive cell. A germ cell is either a male sperm or a female egg. Before puberty, germ cells are similar to other cells and contain a complete number of chromosomes. In humans, this is 46.

Following puberty, hormones in the testes of the male and in the ovaries of the female stimulate the germ cells in order to make them mature for fertilization. In becoming mature, germ cells divide by a process called *meiosis.* When meiosis is complete, each germ cell has 23 chromosomes. This is *half* the number of chromosomes found in all other human cells.

If a mature sperm cell and mature egg cell meet after intercourse, fertilization may occur. When the 23 chromosomes of one germ cell combine with the 23 chromosomes of the other germ cell, the total number is 46. This is the number necessary for beginning the life of a new human being.

See also: **meiosis, ovum, reproduction, sperm, zygote;** Book 2, Chapter 9, *How a Baby Develops*

gestation, see **pregnancy**

going steady Going steady means that a boy and girl or a man and woman date each other exclusively. There are varying opinions as to whether going steady is beneficial to a teenager. Some parents and psychologists think that it helps the young people to establish meaningful relationships. Others think that teenagers should broaden their experience with the opposite sex by dating many people. In the case of men and women, going steady usually leads to engagement and marriage.

See also: **dating**; Book 3, Chapter 18, *Dating for Girls;* Book 3, Chapter 19, *Dating for Boys*

gonads, see **ovaries, testicles**

gonorrhea, see **venereal disease**

growing pains Growing pains is a popular term for the physical discomfort children may feel while they are growing up. When children complain of pains, for example, in their arms or legs, a parent may say without too much concern, "Oh, they're just growing pains." While it is not usual to feel pain from normal body development, sometimes in the years of adolescence the bones will grow faster than the muscles. In such cases, there may be a kind of pulling or stretching feeling until the muscles catch up.

More frequently, growing pains seem to be the result of wearing badly fitted shoes, not getting enough rest, or failing to eat enough of the proper foods while filling up on things like soft drinks and potato chips.

In a few rare cases, pains in the limbs may be symptoms of a disease of the body joints called rheumatic fever.

See also: **adolescence**; Book 1, Chapter 3, *A Boy Becomes a Man;* Book 1, Chapter 4, *A Girl Becomes a Woman*

gynecologist A gynecologist is a physican who specializes in the treatment of women, and especially the female reproductive system. He or she treats any problems or irregularities a woman may have with her menstrual cycle, pregnancy, or menopause. Even when no problems are apparent, it is a good idea for every woman to have an annual examination performed by a gynecologist.

Most gynecologists are also specialists in *obstetrics*, the care of pregnant women.

See also: **obstetrician**

half-brother A half-brother is a male child who has only one parent in common with other children. The son of a woman by her second marriage would be a half-brother to the children by her first marriage, and they would be half-brothers (or half-sisters) to him. The same thing would be true if a father has children by two different marriages. The children of the different marriages would be half-brothers or half-sisters to each other.

hallucinogens, see **drugs**

heredity Heredity is the process by which traits are passed from parents to offspring. It is also the result of that process, for everything a person inherits can be called his "heredity." Heredity and environment together shape one's individuality.

A person's inherited traits come from genes in the reproductive cells of both his mother and father. Mature reproductive cells in humans each contain 23 chromosomes, half the number found in all other human cells. Within each chromosome are genes which determine hair color, eye color, shape of nose, and many other factors.

When chromosomes from the sperm and egg unite during fertilization, the genes combine in a systematic way. At that instant, the inherited traits of the new individual are determined.

See also: **acquired characteristics, chromosome,**

HAIR HEREDITY

environment, gene, inherited characteristics; Book 2, Chapter 13, *Who Will the Baby Be Like*

hermaphrodite A hermaphrodite is an individual who has both male and female sex glands—testicles and ovaries. Such a condition is exceedingly rare.

Some people, called *pseudohermaphrodites*, have both male and female external sex organs in a rudimentary form, but the sex glands of only one sex. Such people are therefore basically either male or female, and they can be helped by a physician to become more completely the sex determined by their glands.

hernia A hernia is a condition in which an organ or tissue protrudes through an opening in its surrounding walls. A commonly used term for hernia is *rupture*.

Hernias usually occur in the abdominal area because of a weakness in body structure. The weakness may be due to a congenital (birth) defect, or it may result from an accident or from tissue that healed poorly following surgery. One common type, *inguinal hernia*, results when abdominal pressure forces a loop of intestine into the scrotum. Frequently this condition will repair itself, but if it does not, medical treatment and/or surgery will be necessary. Treatment depends upon how seriously the health of the individual is affected.

heterosexuality The sexual attraction felt by members of one sex for members of the opposite sex is called heterosexuality. (*Hetero* is a Greek word meaning "other or different.") Such attraction is the basis for the normal relationship between men and women.

See also: **sex appeal, sexuality**

homosexuality Homosexuality is the state in which a person feels a sexual attraction toward someone of his or her own sex. The word homosexuality is formed from the Greek word *homos* which means "the same." Homosexuality is the opposite of heterosexuality, the state of feeling a sexual attraction toward someone of the opposite sex.

Homosexuals are often said to be "queer" or "gay." Other slang words (all of which are derogatory) are *fairy, fag, pansy,* and *queen.* Female homosexuality is generally called *lesbianism* or *sapphism.* A female homosexual is sometimes called a *dike.*

Before puberty almost all boys and girls like people of their own sex best. They may have a crush on a good friend, a teacher, or even an older brother or sister. Sometimes this feeling is somewhat sexual. A crush like this is normal at this time in a child's sexual development.

After puberty, when boys and girls become adolescents, they almost always start feeling attracted to someone of the opposite sex. Suddenly boys want to be close to girls, and girls start dreaming of falling in love with boys.

Homosexuals, however, remain sexually attracted only to people of their same sex. Some people are attracted to both sexes, and this state is called *bisexuality.*

Many people have made studies of homosexuality, but no one really knows why one person becomes a homosexual and another, a heterosexual. Many people think homosexuality may result from the way in which a child is treated by his parents. Other people think homosexuality may sometimes be caused by a physical condition, such as a hormone imbalance. Some homosexuals do develop physical characteristics of the opposite sex. It is also thought that homosexual behavior can be a product either of varying circumstances or of a single situation in a person's life.

Although a homosexual may be an intelligent, kind, and generous person, he or she is not always accepted by other people. In fact, in spite of the gay-rights activists, a homosexual's life in most

societies is still very difficult and sometimes sad.
See also: **bisexual, lesbianism**

hormones A hormone, from the Greek *ormanein* meaning "to excite," is a chemical substance which stimulates activity in the body. Hormones are produced in organs or endocrine glands. They are carried by the blood to other parts of the body where they help to control specific functions.

See also: **adrenal glands, androgens, endocrine glands, estrogens, metabolism, pituitary gland, sex hormones, thyroid gland**

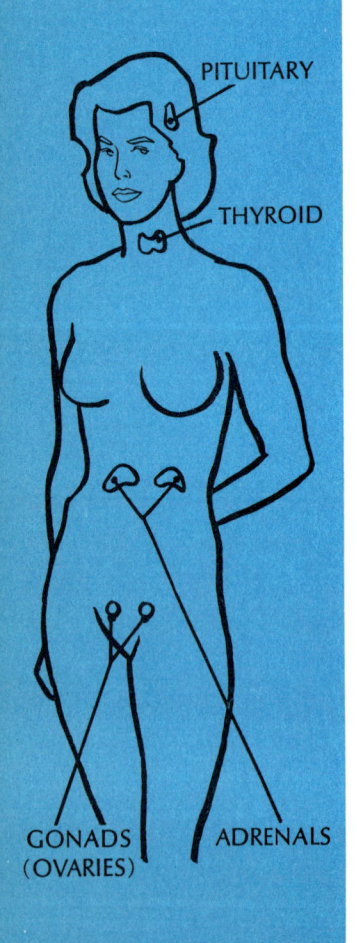

husband A husband is a man joined in marriage with a woman. The word *husband* comes from an Old English word meaning "master of a house."

Husbands at one time held complete control over the household and were responsible for all decisions within the family. In modern society, however, the wife normally enjoys much greater equality with her husband. She, as well as he, has a voice in family decisions. She also enjoys more privileges and holds more responsibilities.

When a man is married, he is legally held to the conditions of his marriage vows. He joins his wife in sharing responsibilities to establish and maintain a household, to be faithful, to have sexual intercourse, and to give care and guidance to children born of the marriage.

It is specifically the husband's legal duty to provide economic support for his wife and children. In many homes today, however, the wife frequently aids in bringing income into the family.

See also: **marriage, wife;** Book 3, Chapter 23, *What About Marriage*

hygiene Hygiene is the practice of good health habits. It includes such things as taking a daily bath or shower, brushing teeth after meals, eating sufficient nutritious food, and getting enough exercise and enough sleep. "Enough" is whatever

HORMONE PRODUCING GLANDS

PITUITARY

THYROID

GONADS (OVARIES)

ADRENALS

amount is necessary to keep the body working without fatigue or illness. Hygiene also includes getting proper medical care for any illness or physical difficulty.

See also: Book 1, Chapter 5, *Feeling Well*

hymen The hymen, or maidenhead, is a membrane that partially closes the opening of the vagina. It connects the labia minora, and has a small opening through which the menstrual flow is discharged. Because the hymen is usually ruptured during the first sexual intercourse, it was previously believed that the absence of the hymen meant that a girl was not a virgin. Now it is known that the hymen can be stretched or ruptured through strenuous exercise or during an examination by a gynecologist. The absence of the hymen, therefore, doesn't always mean that a girl has lost her virginity.

See also: **defloration, labia, virginity**

hysterectomy A hysterectomy is the surgical removal of the uterus. The operation known as *panhysterectomy* means surgical removal of the uterus, Fallopian tubes, and ovaries. These procedures are sometimes referred to as "female operations." Such operations are generally performed only to remedy some abnormality or disease.

Although a woman who has undergone a hysterectomy can no longer have children, she can continue to have normal sexual relations.

See also: **Fallopian tubes, ovaries, uterus**

identical twins, see **multiple birth**

illegitimate child An illegitimate child is one whose parents are not legally married to each other. *Bastard* is the legal term for such a child. If a baby is conceived before a man and woman are married to each other but born after their marriage takes place, he is considered legitimate (legal). If a baby is conceived while his parents are married but born after they are divorced, he is still a legitimate child.

immaturity Immaturity is the state of being not full grown or developed. The word can be applied to any of the three kinds of development—physical, mental, or emotional.

Physical immaturity is easy to see. A baby cannot walk until he has developed the ability to move his legs in coordination with the signals sent from his brain. A person cannot become a weightlifter until his muscles are fully developed.

Mental immaturity is more difficult to see. An individual may be 25 years old and look like any normal adult, but his mental age may be only nine. Only in talking with such a person would his lack of mental development become apparent.

Emotional immaturity is most difficult of all to detect. It means a lack of ability to handle situations and problems that most other people of a given age can deal with. For example, a first grader may need his mother with him when he begins school. Within a few weeks he should normally develop enough independence to stay in class without her. If months pass and the child still cannot be happy at school without his mother, he is considered emotionally immature.

Life is a continual process of growth and development. With the passage of time, immaturity gradually is replaced by maturity. If the process seems to be taking abnormally long in the physical, mental, or emotional area, a physician or psychologist can be consulted for guidance.

See also: **maturation, maturity**

immoral, see **moral**

impotence Impotence is the inability for a male to sustain an erection during sexual intercourse. It can also mean the inability to ejaculate, even though erection is possible. The causes of impotence are usually emotional, but they may be physical in some cases. Anxiety about his sexual capabilities is often the cause of a man's impotence. When anxiety is reduced, chances are that impotence will cease to be a problem. Occasional impotence is not at all unusual.

Impotence should not be confused with sterility. Sterility means that the testes cannot produce sperm capable of fertilizing an egg cell. Men who are sterile can have normal sexual relations.

See also: **ejaculation, erection, potency**

incest Legally, incest means having sexual intercourse with a close blood relative. In a broader sense, it means any kind of sexual relations between relatives. Incest is considered taboo (forbidden) in almost all cultures, and in all religions. The reasons for the taboo are both psychological and medical. Psychologically, acts of incest generally cause very strong guilt feelings. Medically, the children of closely related people would be more likely than other children to inherit any weaknesses present in the family.

incubator An incubator is a specially designed container used to keep premature or sick babies alive. It provides the controlled environment, including proper temperature and oxygen level, that the baby needs. In addition, it helps to keep disease germs away from him.

Premature babies are born before full term, and weigh less than $5^1/_2$ pounds. Because of their small size or early birth, they are unable to adapt to the outside world as quickly as full-term babies. They are placed in incubators until they are ready to live in normal conditions. Some sick babies are also placed in incubators if they need special temperature and oxygen control.

See also: **full-term baby, premature birth**

infatuation Infatuation is an exaggerated feeling

419

of love or admiration for another person. It usually begins quickly, is based on a strong physical attraction, and lasts only a brief time.

A person who is infatuated feels that the person he or she loves is perfect. A person who loves, on the other hand, has a better idea of the personality, ideals, actions, hopes, and fears of the loved one. He realizes that the loved one has both good and bad characteristics.

Although infatuation is considered silly, romantic, or "puppy love," it is a normal feeling that many young people have. It might be considered a stepping-stone toward experiencing a more mature love in later years.

See also: **crush, love, romance**; Book 3, Chapter 22, *How Do You Know When It's Love*

infertility, see **sterility**

inherited characteristics Inherited characteristics are those that pass from one generation to another. They are passed to offspring by means of genes in the mother's egg and the father's sperm. Such characteristics are different from those that are acquired through environment.

Some examples of inherited characteristics are eye color, blood type, hair color and texture, sex, height, and bone structure. A person who inherited genes with the "message" for blond hair and blue eyes will have blond hair and blue eyes.

See also: **acquired characteristics, heredity**; Book 2, Chapter 13, *Who Will the Baby Be Like*

inhibition An inhibition is an inner barrier that stops people from acting according to instinct.

Living in society puts a check on many of mankind's natural instincts. Such control is necessary in order to guarantee that each person's rights are respected. For example, even though a man's instinct is to obtain food when he is hungry, he learns that he cannot take another person's food.

He is inhibited (stopped emotionally) from taking it. Even though a person naturally wishes to act according to instinct in satisfying needs, he is inhibited from doing something that is unacceptable.

The word *inhibition* is often used in referring to sexual matters. Although sexual enjoyment should not be thought of as wrong, some people are taught that it is. This attitude later inhibits normal sexual expression. If a sexually inhibited person marries, he or she might feel it is wrong to respond sexually to his or her spouse. Such a reaction is an example of sexual inhibition.

See also: **instinct**

instinct Instinct is an inborn, natural impulse that causes animals and human beings to act in certain ways without being taught.

Animals seem to know by instinct where and how to find food, water, and shelter. They instinctively migrate or hibernate to protect themselves from harmful weather changes. They know how to protect themselves from almost any danger.

Animals also instinctively know, once their bodies are mature, how to mate and give birth to offspring. They follow the natural manner and cycle of reproduction common to their species.

See also: **inhibition**; Book 1, Chapter 1, *The Life Cycle*

intercourse, see **sexual intercourse**

intrauterine device, see **contraception**

jealousy Jealousy is an emotion a person may experience if he feels insecure and inadequate. Insecurity causes one to feel threatened by and jealous of anyone who seems to be superior.

For example, a boy may feel jealousy when he sees his girl friend talking to another boy. He becomes suspicious and afraid that he will lose her affection.

L

Jealousy is often caused by envy. A girl may be envious of a friend's good grades in school, and envy may turn into jealousy.

Jealousy is a normal emotion. Everyone feels jealousy at some time in his life. However, jealousy can make people miserable. It can make them so untrusting and hostile that they cannot get along with other people. Jealousy can be controlled if a person has confidence in himself. A confident person does not doubt the love and respect of other people. Rather, he feels worthy of it.

See also: Book 2, Chapter 15, *A Baby Makes a Family*

jockstrap A jock (or jockey) strap is a device worn around the pelvic area by boys and men to protect their genitals. This strap is usually made of elastic cotton cloth, and it supports the genitals during sports and other strenuous activities. Another name for a jockstrap is *athletic supporter.*

See also: **reproductive organs**

labia Labia are the folds of skin in a girl's or woman's external genital area, the vulva. The word *labia* is the plural of *labium,* meaning lip, which describes each one of these folds. They are sometimes called the *vaginal lips.*

There are two sets of labia. *Labia majora* are the two larger folds on the outside of the genital area. They give protection to the vaginal and urinary openings, as well as to the labia minora. *Labia minora,* smaller folds of skin closer to the body, cover the clitoris and vaginal opening.

See also: **vulva**

labor Labor is the name given to the uterine contractions and other processes of childbirth. A female in the act of having a baby is "in labor."

The birth process can be divided into three stages of labor. The first stage of labor includes the uterine contractions which push the baby toward the opening (cervix) of the uterus. The second stage is the passage of the baby through the birth canal and his actual birth. The delivery of the placenta and other afterbirth tissues is the third stage of labor.

Labor normally begins about nine months after a baby's conception. The muscles of a woman's uterus start to contract, gradually pushing the baby against the cervix. The frequency of contractions increases from one about every half hour at the beginning of labor to one about every two or three minutes at the end of the first stage of labor.

These contractions, often called *labor pains*, push the baby down toward the cervix, causing the cervix to dilate, or open. The first stage of labor is over when the cervix has opened up enough to allow the baby's head to pass through. By this time most women have gone to the hospital and are under the care of a doctor and nurses.

Some time during the first stage of labor the membranes surrounding the baby rupture. (These are the membranes of the amniotic sac in which the baby floated while he developed.) When the membranes rupture, it is said that a woman's "bag of waters" has broken. Occasionally the membranes rupture before labor begins. In other cases a doctor may have to rupture the membranes.

The second stage of labor begins when the baby passes out of the uterus and starts down the birth canal. His mother continues having muscle contractions that help push him along. Sometimes a doctor will give medication to a woman to ease some of the discomfort of labor.

Most babies are born head first. When the baby's head appears, the doctor is ready to help guide the baby out of his mother's body.

The third stage of labor occurs after the baby is born. The uterus continues to contract and its surface gets smaller. This causes the placenta to fall away from the uterine lining, and the contractions force the afterbirth to pass out of the woman's body. The uterus bleeds a little while it empties itself, but as it shrinks back to a normal size, the bleeding stops. Once the uterus is empty, the muscle contractions stop and labor is ended. A woman is taken from the delivery room and rests a while before she starts to care for her new baby.

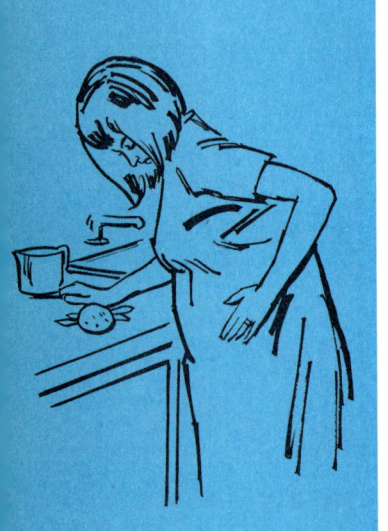

See also: **amnion, birth, natural childbirth, placenta, uterus, vagina;** Book 2, Chapter 11, *How a Baby Is Born*

lactation, see **breast feeding**

lesbianism Lesbianism is female homosexuality. The word lesbianism comes from the name of the Greek island, Lesbos. A Greek poetess named Sappho once lived on Lesbos. Sappho was the leader of a group of women who were very much interested in the arts. Some people believed that Sappho and her friends practiced homosexuality. Therefore, the island Lesbos, on which they lived, gave its name to this type of sexual behavior.

See also: **bisexual, homosexuality**

leukorrhea, see **vaginal discharge**

life cycle Cycle comes from the Greek word *kyklos*, meaning circle or wheel. Just as a circle has neither beginning nor end, the life cycle of a species cannot be said to start or finish at a certain point. The life cycle of an individual is the process in accordance with which it is born, becomes mature, reproduces its own kind, and eventually dies, leaving the young to continue the cycle. Whether we speak of a daisy or a dog, a mayfly or a man, the basic fact of life is that only living things can produce new living things. The way in which each of the various kinds of plants and animals carries out its life cycle is one of the things that makes each species unique.

See also: **reproduction;** Book 1, Chapter 1, *The Life Cycle;* Book 2, Chapter 8, *The Beginning of a Life Cycle*

love Love is a feeling of extreme affection, tenderness, and devotion. Love is a complex emotion; a person who loves puts many of the desires and cares of his loved ones above his own needs.

There are many different kinds of love. Self-love is thought to be the first kind of love every person feels. A small baby learns to love himself and his own body before he feels love for other people. Children later learn to love their parents. They also learn to love many people outside their families.

At puberty love becomes influenced by sexual desire. Although some people base their love on sexual drive alone, most people realize that love involves more than sex.

See also: **crush, infatuation, platonic love, romance**; Book 3, Chapter 22, *How Do You Know When It's Love*

lover The term *lover* is usually used to describe someone who is in love with another person. Lover can apply to either a husband or a wife. However, the most popular use of the word lover is to describe unmarried people who are in love. People who have an extramarital affair, involving sexual intercourse, are also called lovers.

See also: **mistress**

LSD, see **drugs**

maidenhead, see **hymen**

making love Making love is a popular term for sexual intercourse. Making love includes all of the love play which leads up to the actual sex act, and to that act itself.

To make love implies more than a physical act. It means that human emotions are involved.

See also: **sexual intercourse**

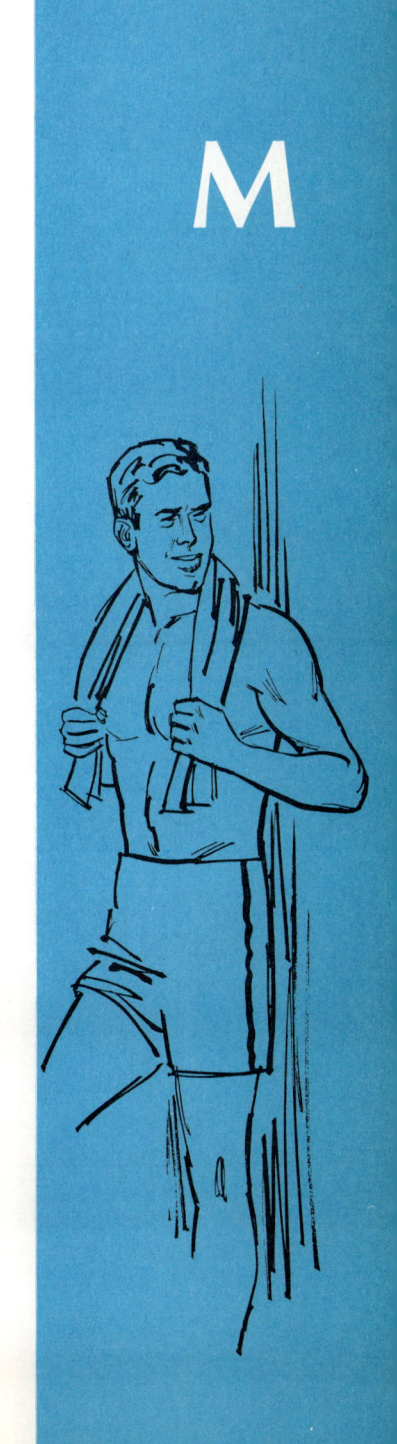

making out Making out is a popular term for sex play. The term *making out* is most often used by adolescents. It generally means kissing and necking. However, making out can also include petting and even sexual intercourse.

See also: **necking, petting;** Book 3, Chapter 20, *Necking, Petting, and Sexual Feelings*

male In all forms of life that continue their species by sexual reproduction, the male is the parent that produces the fertilizing agent. In plants the substance is called *pollen;* in animals it is called *sperm.*

In all mammals, including human beings, the sperm fertilizes the female egg to continue the life cycle. Fertilization begins the life of a new individual. The male is the father of the offspring.

The word *male* also refers to all physical organs, traits, and characteristics found only in the male sex. In human beings, these are the things that contribute to an individual's masculinity.

See also: **masculinity;** Book 1, Chapter 3, *A Boy Becomes a Man*

male reproductive system, see **reproductive organs**

mammal A mammal is an animal belonging to the most highly developed class of all living beings. Human beings are included in this classification.

Although the word *mammal* includes many animals in one large category, mammals vary greatly in size, shape, and ways of living. A tiny mouse is a mammal. So is a gigantic whale.

Mammals are alike in the following ways:

1) All female mammals feed their young with milk that comes from mammary glands. The word *mammal* comes from the Latin word *mamma* which means "milk."

2) Fertilization occurs inside the female's body.

3) Almost all mammals give birth to live young. (The only exceptions are two egg-laying mammals—the duck-billed platypus and a rare species of spiny anteaters.) Mammals are superior to other animals in the care and protection of their young.

4) All mammals breathe air by using lungs. They are warm-blooded and can adjust to temperature changes.

5) All mammals have backbones.

6) All mammals have either fur or hair.

See also: Book 1, Chapter 2, *The Miracle of Growth*

mammary glands, see **breast feeding, breasts**

marijuana, see **drugs**

marital   Marital is a word referring to marriage. For example, problems that married people might have are sometimes called *marital difficulties*. Something occurring before marriage is called *premarital*. A love affair between a man and woman in addition to the marriage of either is *extramarital*.

marriage   Marriage, or *matrimony*, is the socially approved, legal union of a man and woman who establish a household and live together as husband and wife. In almost all societies, this union is begun by some social, legal, or religious ceremony. When a man and woman marry, they agree to accept the duties and privileges of husband and wife according to their particular society or culture.

In the United States and other similar cultures, a marriage is considered successful if it brings personal satisfaction and happiness to each partner. In these societies, where individuals select their own mates, young people have many opportunities to meet members of the opposite sex. They usually select a marital partner who shares similar beliefs and goals in life, who is a good companion, and who satisfies their personal (sexual and psychological) needs. Love and mutual respect, as well as economic stability, are considered important to a marriage.

Marriage in the United States is legally governed by the laws of each state. A man and woman who wish to marry obtain a marriage license and are later married by either a civil official, such as a judge or justice of the peace, or by a church official: a minister, priest, or rabbi, or by both. Witnesses observe the ceremony and the official makes a written record of the marriage. Both the husband and wife are legally held to the conditions of their marriage vows, spoken in the ceremony, as long as they are married.

See also: **annulment, divorce, engagement, husband, monogamy, wife;** Book 3, Chapter 23, *What About Marriage*

marriage license A marriage license is a document which states that a man and woman have been given legal authority to marry. The license is obtained by couples intending to marry, and it is then given to the official performing the marriage ceremony.

Certain conditions must exist before legal permission to marry is given. One condition is that the couple is of the legal age for marriage according to that state's law, or that parents have consented to the marriage if the young people are under age. Another condition is that neither of the partners is presently married to another person.

In many states, evidence of a blood test must be shown before a marriage license is given. These blood tests give proof that neither of the partners has a venereal disease which could be harmful to children born of that marriage.

masculinity Masculinity is the total of those attributes that characterize men rather than women. It is expected that a man will have a larger body build, a deeper voice, and greater physical strength than a woman. Aggressiveness and fearlessness have usually been considered masculine traits. In recent years many people in the United States and similar societies have changed their opinions about what is masculine or feminine. Now we see that both sexes can—and should—feel and express such traits as tenderness (feminine) and courage (masculine).

See also: **femininity, sexuality;** Book 1, Chapter 3, *A Boy Becomes a Man*

masochism Masochism refers to the attainment of sexual pleasure through being abused or dominated. The word comes from the name of a German novelist, Leopold von Sacher-Masoch, who both practiced and wrote about the abnormality.

See also: **sadism**

masturbation Masturbation is the act of touching or rubbing one's own genitals and getting sexual stimulation from the touch. Masturbation is sometimes called "playing with yourself."

Almost everyone masturbates at some time in his or her life. Babies usually find out that touching their genitals causes a pleasant feeling. When children reach puberty, they have many new sexual urges. They sometimes satisfy these urges by masturbating.

Some people, especially adolescents, have been taught to be ashamed of their sexual urges. When they have these feelings and masturbate, they feel a strong sense of guilt. This guilt can be harmful to a person's emotional health. No one should be embarrassed by sexual urges because these feelings are a part of being human.

In the past masturbation was thought to be harmful to a person's health. It was believed to cause such disorders as acne, blindness, and insanity. Today, however, we know that masturbation is not harmful. It does not cause any physical or mental disorder.

See also: Book 1, Chapter 3, *A Boy Becomes a Man;* Book 3, Chapter 20, *Necking, Petting, and Sexual Feelings*

mate A mate is one of a pair. In living beings, a

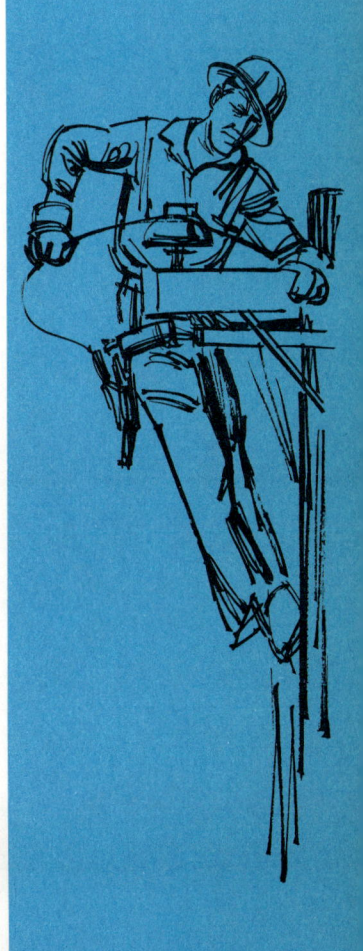

mate is the one of the opposite sex with whom another pairs for reproductive purposes. A husband is the mate of the wife, and the wife is the mate of the husband. In other living forms, the male and female are called mates as long as they stay together to reproduce.

To *mate* means to have sexual intercourse.

See also: Book 1, Chapter 1, *The Life Cycle;* Book 1, Chapter 2, *The Miracle of Growth*

maternal Maternal refers to characteristics associated with mothers. It includes feelings which cause a mother to act in a certain way toward her offspring. It also includes other terms related to a mother, such as maternal side of the family (the mother's parents, sisters and brothers, and so on), maternal duties, and maternal instincts.

Most mothers in higher forms of life have maternal instincts. These are inner drives which cause mothers to feed, care for, and protect their young.

See also: **instinct, paternal**

maternity Maternity refers to motherhood. It especially refers to the time a woman is pregnant or just after she has given birth to a baby.

During pregnancy, the term *maternity* is applied to special loose-fitting clothes that a woman wears as the baby grows inside her. Later, when a woman is in the hospital to give birth to her baby, she is placed in the maternity ward, an area especially for new babies and their mothers.

See also: **pregnancy, prenatal care;** Book 2, Chapter 10, *The Mother of the Baby*

maturation Maturation is the process of growing and developing toward adulthood. Maturation normally occurs according to time schedules or stages that are specific for every cell, plant, animal, and human being.

In humans, the first stage of maturation begins the moment an egg and sperm unite and begin developing into a baby. From the time of birth, maturation includes the stages of growth that occur during childhood, puberty, and adolescence.

The most noticeable stage of maturation occurs around puberty. At this time, reproductive organs begin to develop and secondary sex characteristics appear. This maturation, plus the additional development that occurs during the remaining years of adolescence, results in boys and girls becoming adult men and women.

See also: **adolescence, adult, puberty**; Book 1, Chapter 3, *A Boy Becomes a Man*; Book 1, Chapter 4, *A Girl Becomes a Woman*

maturity Maturity usually describes the condition of a cell, plant, animal, or human being which has reached full adult growth and development. In humans, the term also describes a person who has developed the mental and emotional qualities of an adult man or woman.

In referring to the life cycle, a cell, plant, animal, or human must be sexually mature before reproduction can occur. For example, germ cells (sperms and eggs) are not mature until they have gone through the cell division of meiosis. Only when they are mature can they join with each other to begin the life of a new individual. Human beings are not sexually mature until their reproductive organs have completely developed.

In referring to the complete maturity of human beings, emotional and mental maturity are also included. Emotional maturity is a person's ability to react to problems and situations in a positive, responsible way. Mental maturity is the ability to think and reason in a logical, intelligent way, applying knowledge and experience gained. Emotional and mental maturity take many more years to develop than does physical maturity.

See also: **adult, immaturity**

meiosis Meiosis is the basic way in which germ cells (sperm and egg) divide while becoming mature for fertilization. After meiosis, a germ cell has *half* the number of chromosomes necessary to continue life of that species. If a mature sperm joins with a mature egg, together they will have the *total* number of chromosomes necessary to begin the life of a new individual. In humans, this number is 46. A mature sperm cell and egg cell each have 23 chromosomes.

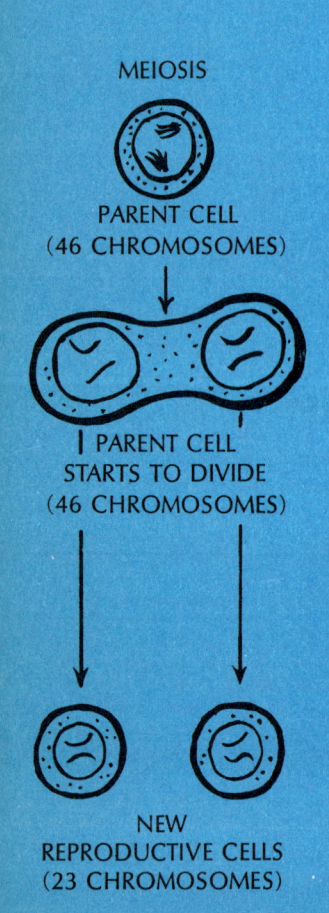

See also: **cell, chromosome, fertilization, germ cell, mitosis;** Book 2, Chapter 13, *Who Will the Baby Be Like*

menarche, see **menstruation**

menopause Menopause is the time in a woman's life when her menstrual periods end and her ovaries stop releasing ova (eggs). It usually occurs when a woman is between the ages of 45 and 50. Other names for the menopause are *change of life* and *climacteric.*

Menopause can be considered the opposite of puberty. During puberty, sex hormones begin to stimulate the periodic occurrence of menstruation and ovulation. This enables a woman to conceive and bear children for many years. During menopause, the release of sex hormones gradually slows down and the entire menstrual cycle eventually ends. When menopause has ended, a woman can no longer give birth to a child.

See also: **menstruation, ovulation, sex hormones**

menstruation Menstruation is the normal, periodic discharge of bloody fluid from the uterus through the vagina. It is also commonly called the "period," or the "curse," and is referred to as the *menses.*

Menstruation is one part of the menstrual, or reproductive, cycle. The menstrual cycle is regulated by female sex hormones.

Menstruation marks the beginning of the menstrual cycle. Half way through this cycle ovulation occurs—an egg is released by one of the two

MEIOSIS

PARENT CELL
(46 CHROMOSOMES)

1 PARENT CELL
STARTS TO DIVIDE
(46 CHROMOSOMES)

NEW
REPRODUCTIVE CELLS
(23 CHROMOSOMES)

ovaries. While an ovary is preparing to release an egg, it gives off a hormone. This hormone causes the uterus to build up a rich lining of blood and tissue to receive the egg. If the released egg is fertilized by a sperm, it will attach itself to this lining and develop into a baby. However, if the egg is not fertilized, it will wither and pass out of a female's body. With it will go the uterine lining which is no longer needed. Menstruation is this "shedding" of the uterine lining and the egg. The total menstrual flow is about four ounces.

A girl's first menstruation is called her *menarche.* The menarche, which usually occurs between the ages of 10 and 14, signifies that a girl has reached puberty. Some girls have their first menstrual discharge at the age of nine, and others may be 16 or even 18 before they first menstruate.

Menstruation normally occurs about every 28 days. However, it is common for a girl to skip a few months between the times of her first few menstrual periods.

During a girl's first few menstrual periods, an egg may not be released. Sometimes the ovaries do not start releasing an egg every month until a girl has been menstruating for a year or more. It takes time for a menstrual cycle to become regulated.

All girls' menstrual cycles are different. It may be normal for one girl to menstruate every 25 days and have a very light flow lasting only two or three days. But it is also normal for another girl to have her period every 35 days, and have a heavy flow that lasts for a week. Lack of any menstrual flow is called *amenorrhea.* Such a condition in a girl 16 or older should be reported to a physician.

There are two kinds of sanitary protection to trap the menstrual flow. A *sanitary pad* is a pad made of layers of absorbent cotton that a girl wears between her legs and over the opening of her vagina. This pad, held in place by a *sanitary belt,* absorbs the menstrual fluid. A *tampon* is a small roll of absorbent material that is inserted into the vagina where it soaks up the fluid. Using a tampon does not affect a girl's virginity.

For a few days before menstruation a girl's breasts may be very sensitive, and she may have a small pain in her back and an extra pimple or two on her face. She may also be irritable or depressed. These discomforts are part of what is called *premenstrual tension.*

Some girls complain of cramps in the lower abdomen during their periods. Pain accompanying menstruation is called *dysmenorrhea.* Cramps are probably caused by the muscle contractions of the uterus as it sheds its lining. Cramps are normal, but if they become too painful, a girl can talk to her doctor. He can prescribe drugs and suggest exercises to help ease the discomfort of cramps.

A woman does not menstruate all her life. Around the age of 45 to 50 she experiences the *change of life* or *menopause*—the stopping of her menstrual periods.

Menstruation is a dramatic sign that a girl is becoming a mature woman. It should be expected and welcomed as a normal part of being a female.

See also: **menopause, ovulation;** Book 1, Chapter 4, *A Girl Becomes a Woman*

mental retardation, see **birth defect**

metabolism Metabolism is the process by which living things build and repair their bodies and produce energy. Metabolism comes from the Greek word meaning "to change." Metabolism can be thought of as tissue change. In metabolism the body's cells are continually building up and breaking down the body's tissues.

Just as a furnace needs fuel to burn and make heat, so the body must have food to build tissues and to produce energy for life. Food is the basic material for all processes of metabolism.

The foods a person eats are made up of special nutrients which the cells use. The basic nutrients are water, proteins, fats, carbohydrates, minerals, and vitamins. After a person eats these nutrients, they are broken down and prepared for the body's cells by the digestive system.

The cells absorb these predigested foods. Some of this food is oxidized or burned by the cells to produce energy. The body always needs energy to live, whether one is eating, walking, or sleeping.

See also: **diet, nutrition, thyroid gland**

midwife A midwife is a woman who helps a mother during the delivery of her baby. The practice of midwifery began very early in history, when women first volunteered to make childbirth easier for both the mother and child. As society became more advanced, laws required that midwives have special training and pass examinations before being licensed to assist at births.

In the United States and in most other modern countries, midwifery has been largely replaced by *obstetrics,* the medical field dealing with the scientific management of women during pregnancy.

The modern day "midwife" in the U.S. is a Certified Nurse Midwife. She is a Registered Nurse (R.N.) with additional special training in obstetrics. Usually she is employed in a hospital or clinic as part of the obstetrical team, which also includes the obstetrician, anesthesiologist, and nurses.

See also: **obstetrician**

minor A minor is a person who has not reached legal adult age, usually 21 years. When a person is 21 years old, he or she is said to have "reached the age of consent" or "attained majority."

Passing the twenty-first birthday does not automatically mean that a young man or woman is mature. It is necessary, however, that some age be recognized as the legal beginning of adulthood, when the young person can accept the privileges and responsibilities of being a citizen.

See also: **adult**

miscarriage A miscarriage, or "miss," is the natural expulsion of a fetus from a uterus through the vagina. A miscarriage usually occurs if something has interfered with the normal growth of the fetus. It is nature's way of discarding a fetus which would probably not develop into a normal, healthy baby.

A miscarriage might occur if an embryo is not attached properly to the wall of the uterus. It might occur if a healthy germ cell was not formed when the sperm and egg united. These and other natural factors cause miscarriages in approximately 10 percent of all pregnancies.

See also: **abortion**

mistress The term *mistress* is used to describe women in two general ways. Mistress is often used to describe a woman who has authority or control over a house, establishment, or institution. Used in this way, a wife is called "the mistress of the household." A woman who is in control of a certain school might also be called "the mistress."

Mistress is also used to describe a woman who has a continuous intimate sexual relationship with a man to whom she is not married. For example, if a man and woman were living together but were not married to each other, the woman might be called the man's mistress.

See also: **lover**

mitosis Mitosis is the basic way in which cells of most live things divide in order to form new cells. It is the method of division that continues the life cycle of most plant, animal, and human cells *except* germ cells. Germ cells (sperm and egg) divide through a process called *meiosis*.

In mitosis, each cell divides creating two new cells, each of which has the same chromosome type and number as the parent cell. Genes in the chromosomes carry to the new cells characteristics identical to those found in the original cell.

See also: **cell, chromosome, gene, germ cell,**

meiosis; Book 2, Chapter 13, *Who Will the Baby Be Like*

monogamy Monogamy is the form of marriage in which each partner is married to only one person at a time. This is the legal form of marriage in the United States and in most societies.

The word *monogamy* comes from the Greek words meaning *act of marrying one*. In a society where monogamy is enforced, neither a husband nor wife can legally marry another person while still married to the first spouse. If a person marries a second spouse while validly married to another, the act is called *bigamy*, and it is a crime.

Monogamy is in contrast to another form of marriage, *polygamy*, which is practiced in some societies. Polygamy is the form of marriage in which a spouse can legally be married to two or more wives or husbands at the same time.

See also: **marriage**

mons veneris Mons veneris means "mound of Venus." Another term for mons veneris is *mons pubis*. It is the mound of fatty tissue covered with skin that is at the base of the abdomen between the thighs. It forms the front part of a girl's or woman's external genital area (the vulva). After puberty, the mons is covered with hair.

monthly period, see **menstruation**

moral Moral means that which is good and right according to the standards of a particular society. *Morals* are the guiding principles people are expected to live by. *Morality* is the entire body of ideas about what is right. The philosophical consideration of morality is called *ethics*.

In Western civilization, morality is based upon what is known as the Judaeo-Christian tradition; that is, the ideas embodied in the Old and New Testaments of the Bible and set forth specifically

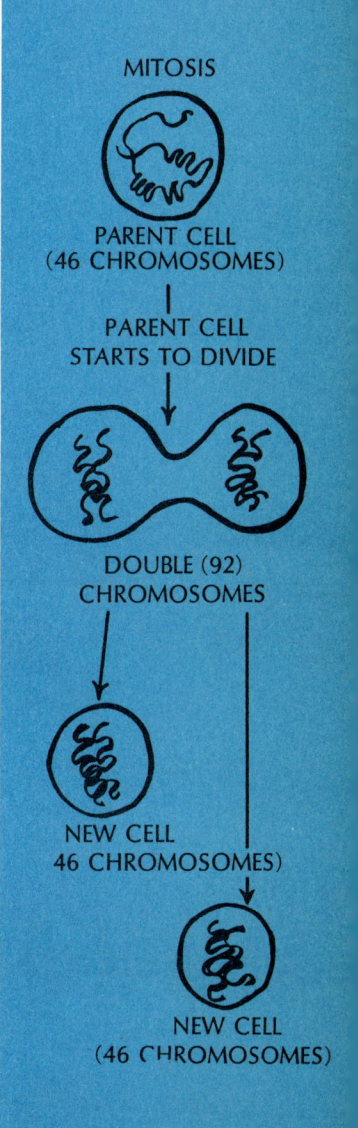

MITOSIS

PARENT CELL
(46 CHROMOSOMES)

PARENT CELL
STARTS TO DIVIDE

DOUBLE (92)
CHROMOSOMES

NEW CELL
46 CHROMOSOMES)

NEW CELL
(46 CHROMOSOMES)

in the Ten Commandments. It is wrong, for example, to steal, to lie, and to commit adultery. A person who knows these things are wrong and does them anyway is acting *immorally (im* means *not).* A person who never learned the rules or who is incapable of understanding them may act in an *amoral* manner *(a* means *without).*

Some people think that society is changing many of its ideas about what is moral and what is immoral, and that a "new morality" is developing. It cannot be said for certain whether individual morality is really changing or whether more and more people are simply choosing to act openly without regard for the established morality standards.

There *is* a new development in social morality. Many people now believe that poverty, famine, disease, war, and persecution are not merely unfortunate but actually immoral conditions, and that society has a moral duty to end them.

See also: Book 1, Chapter 7, *You Are An Individual*

morning sickness Morning sickness is the name given to the feelings of nausea frequently experienced by women during the early months of pregnancy. Medical opinion on the causes of morning sickness varies. Some physicians feel it is psychological; others feel there are real physical causes.

See also: **pregnancy, prenatal care**

multiple birth In humans, a multiple birth is the birth of two or more infants during the same time of labor. The term *multiple birth* is used chiefly in referring to humans and other mammals, such as horses, cows, and monkeys, which usually give birth to only one offspring during the same labor.

Other female animals, such as cats and dogs, normally give birth to two or more offspring during one time of labor. The term used in referring to multiple offspring of these animals is *litter.*

A multiple birth in humans may result in two infants (twins); three infants (triplets); four infants (quadruplets); five infants (quintuplets); or, in extremely rare cases, six (sextuplets) or seven infants (septuplets).

According to birth records, the chance that a woman will give birth to twins is about one in 90 births. The birth of triplets occurs about once in every 10,000 births. Only about two sets of quadruplets are born in a million births. Quintuplets are even more rare and occur only about ten times in an entire century. The chance that a woman will give birth to a set of quintuplets is about 40 million to one! Sextuplets and septuplets occur so seldom that no ratio of their birth has been listed.

There are two causes of multiple birth. Each results in a different type of offspring: either identical or fraternal.

Identical infants result when a single fertilized egg divides into two, three, or more completely new cells before beginning embryonic development. If the egg divides into two new cells, twins will develop; if it divides into three new cells, triplets will result. As these new cells begin to develop into babies, they grow closely together and usually share the same placenta.

Since identical infants carry similar genes from the same fertilized egg, they are almost exactly alike. They are of the same sex and have the same blood type and general physical characteristics.

Fraternal infants may result if more than one egg is released from the ovaries during ovulation. Each egg that is fertilized by a different sperm will then begin to develop into a new human being. If two eggs are released and fertilized, twins may develop; if three eggs are released and fertilized, triplets may develop.

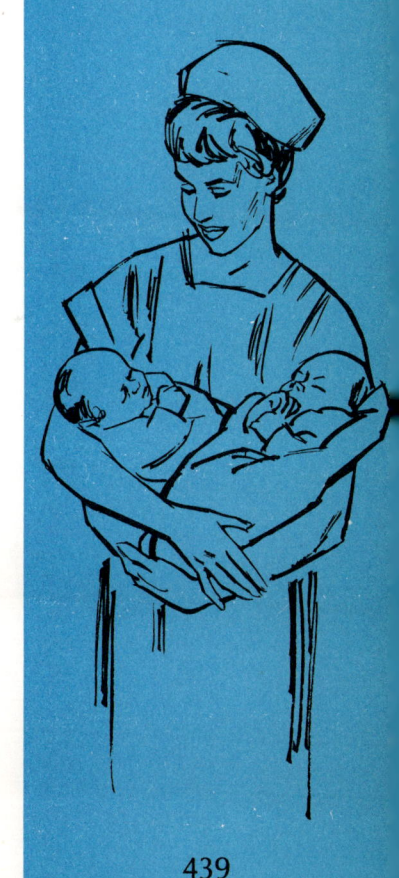

Since fraternal infants in a multiple birth result from two or more entirely different egg-sperm combinations, they do not have the same hereditary genes. They will differ as much as brothers and sisters born at different times do. They may be of either the same sex or of different sexes; they might have different blood types; and they will have different physical characteristics.

Multiple births of triplets, quadruplets, or quintuplets can result in a combination of both identical and fraternal infants. For example, if two eggs released during ovulation are fertilized, one may begin embryonic development, and the other may split into two entirely different cells. The result will be two identical infants and one fraternal (nonidentical) infant. There are various possible combinations of multiple birth babies.

narcotics, see **drugs**

natural childbirth Natural childbirth is a general term used to describe childbirth in which a woman is an active participant, rather than being completely anesthetized.

In preparing for natural childbirth, a woman usually learns as much as she can about the birth process. She reads about it and sometimes attends classes on childbirth. One might think that "natural childbirth" means that delivery of the baby "just happens," but the theory of natural childbirth says that the more a woman knows about the way a baby is born, the easier delivery will be for her. She will know what to expect and, therefore, she will be able to take part more fully in the birth process.

A woman interested in experiencing natural childbirth often practices breathing and relaxing techniques to use during labor. These techniques will help her to use her muscles and "work with" the uterine contractions. Some doctors encourage their patients to experience natural childbirth; others prefer to rely on medical techniques.

See also: **birth, labor;** Book 2, Chapter 11, *How a Baby Is Born*

navel The navel is the small indentation in the middle of the abdomen, usually called the "belly button." It is the place where the umbilical cord was attached to the body before birth.

See also: **umbilical cord**

necking Necking is light sex play. The word means different things to different people. Generally, necking is thought of as kissing, hugging, and other sex play between two people that may or may not arouse strong sexual feelings in either one.

See also: Book 3, Chapter 20, *Necking, Petting, and Sexual Feelings*

nipple, see **breasts**

nocturnal emission, see **seminal emission**

normal Normal, from the Latin *norma*, meaning *rule*, refers to something that is typical or that serves as a general rule. In the life cycle, the word *normal* refers to physical appearances, body functions, and behavior that are common within a given species. An action or situation called normal is what occurs in the majority of cases within species or social groups.

In describing human beings it is difficult to define exactly what is normal. Every individual, with his own complex genetic and environmental background, differs from every other. Although a certain trait may be normal within one individual or one society, it may be considered abnormal, or uncommon, in another.

A person is *physically* normal if he has the appearance of a human being and is free from diseases, infections, or malformations. A person born with three arms would be considered abnormal.

Normal *body functions* are those that operate in the correct way, enabling a person to eat, digest food, breathe, and reproduce. If a body organ fails to perform its task properly, it is said to be functioning abnormally.

Normal *behavior*, defined psychologically, is

found in a person with the intelligence, emotional reactions, and personality traits that are commonly noted in a particular society or age group. It is normal for a baby to cry when he is hungry. This is expected and is common for his age. In most cases, though, it is not normal for an adult to cry when he is hungry.

See also: **abnormal**; Book 1, Chapter 6, *What Is Normal?*

nursing, see **breast feeding**

nutrition Nutrition means nourishing the body. Good nutrition is based on a well-balanced diet that satisfies the daily nutrient requirements for a person's body needs. It supplies the proteins, minerals, vitamins, calories, and other things that are necessary for that person's proper body function and growth. A person with *malnutrition* has an unbalanced diet that lacks necessary foods.

Nutrition is also the name of the science dealing with food and its relationship to the health of human beings and animals. Through studies in nutrition, it has been learned that children, teenagers, and pregnant women need special diets to satisfy the special demands of their time of life.

See also: **diet, metabolism**; Book 1, Chapter 5, *Feeling Well*

nymphomania Nymphomania is a rare condition in which a woman has an uncontrollable sex drive. Such a woman, called a *nymphomaniac*, has a constant urge to have sexual intercourse.

Nymphomania may be caused by emotional factors. Some women can be cured of nymphomania by psychological counseling.

Women have different levels of sexual desire. In some women it is very strong. The strong sex drive of normal women is not the same thing as nymphomania, which is uncontrollable.

A similar condition in men is called *satyriasis*.
See also: **sex drive**

obscenity An obscenity is something that is offensive to modesty or decency. What is considered obscee depends upon a society's accepted standards of morality. One society may consider any representation of the sex act obscene, while another will find acts of violence indecent. Obscene words, pictures, or acts are those considered by the majority of people to be disgusting or shocking.
See also: **moral, pornography**

obstetrician An obstetrician is a physician who cares for a woman during pregnancy, childbirth, and for about three to six weeks following delivery. He or she has specialized in obstetrics, the medical science concerned with care and treatment of mothers and their babies. Such medical training enables the obstetrician to make birth easier and safer for both the mother and baby. An obstetrician is usually also a gynecologist, a specialist who cares for the special health problems of women. The name *obstetrician* comes from the Latin *obstetrix* which means "midwife."
See also: **gynecologist, midwife, prenatal care**

oil glands Oil glands, or *sebaceous glands*, are tiny exocrine glands which secrete an oily substance called *sebum* through the pores to the surface of the skin. Sebum helps keep hair from becoming dry or brittle, it helps maintain the moisture of skin, and it protects the body from losing too much body fluid through absorption or evaporation through the skin.

During puberty, the sebaceous glands are greatly influenced by the increase of androgens (male sex hormones) circulating in the bodies of both boys and girls. These androgens, which aid in producing the characteristic rougher skin of males, also increase the size and activity of the oil glands.

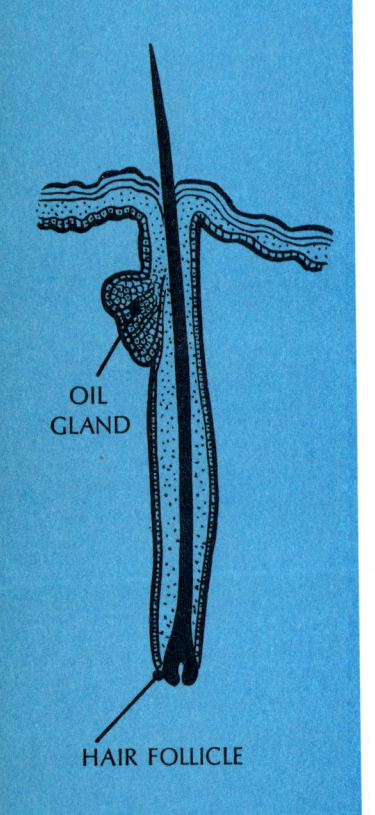

With the increase of sebum coming from these glands, there is frequently a clogging of sebum at the opening of the pore. This clogging causes the pimples, blackheads, or boils characteristic of *acne*.

Although acne is most common in boys during adolescence, it also frequently occurs in girls. A girl's sex hormones are primarily estrogens (female sex hormones) which help to keep her skin soft and clear, but she also has a certain amount of androgens. They are especially active just before or during menstruation, when her estrogen level is low. Androgen activity at the time of menstruation is the reason for the appearance of pimples.

See also: **acne, androgens, dermatologist, estrogens, exocrine glands**

oral contraceptive, see **contraception**

orgasm Orgasm is the climax of sexual excitement. It is the final burst of pleasurable feeling which accompanies the release of muscular and nervous tension at the end of a sex act. For both men and women, the sensation of orgasm is centered in the pelvic region: penis and testicles in men, clitoris, vagina, and uterus in women. In the male, ejaculation of semen accompanies orgasm. In the female, there is no comparable ejaculation. A woman does not have to experience orgasm in order to conceive. Orgasm can also result from masturbation or petting.

See also: **sexual intercourse**

ovaries Ovary comes from a Latin word meaning "an egg holder." Ovaries are female reproductive glands which produce eggs. Ovaries also produce hormones which control the regulation of a female's reproductive cycle and the secondary sex characteristics.

Every woman has two ovaries, each about the size and shape of an almond. They are on each side of the uterus. Eggs move from the ovaries to the uterus through passages called Fallopian tubes.

Although ovaries are small, they contain thousands of tiny, undeveloped eggs at the time of a girl's birth. A girl's body does not produce any more eggs after birth. The eggs are contained in tiny pouches along the ovary walls.

When a girl reaches the age of puberty, her ovaries become active. Undeveloped eggs begin to mature. Once a month, an egg in one of the ovaries is ready for fertilization and is started on its journey to the uterus. If it is fertilized, pregnancy will begin. If it is not fertilized, it will be disposed of in the process of menstruation.

When *menopause* occurs, at age 45 to 50, the ovaries stop releasing eggs. The supply of female hormones also is less.

See also: **menstruation, ovulation, ovum, pregnancy, sex hormones**

ovulation Ovulation is the part of the reproductive cycle during which a mature egg is released from one of the ovaries. A woman usually ovulates about every 28 days, between about the 10th and 14th days of the menstrual cycle, from the time of puberty until menopause.

During each cycle, hormones in the ovaries stimulate one of the undeveloped eggs to grow. As the egg matures, it goes through a special cell division called meiosis. When meiosis is complete, the egg has 23 chromosomes, half the number necessary for human life.

As meiosis is taking place, fluid accumulates around the egg. When the egg is completely "ripe," this fluid causes the egg to burst out of the ovary. This release is ovulation.

Following ovulation, the egg enters the Fallopian tube near it. The egg then travels slowly through the tube to the uterus. If it meets with a mature sperm in the Fallopian tube, fertilization may occur. The 23 chromosomes of the mature egg

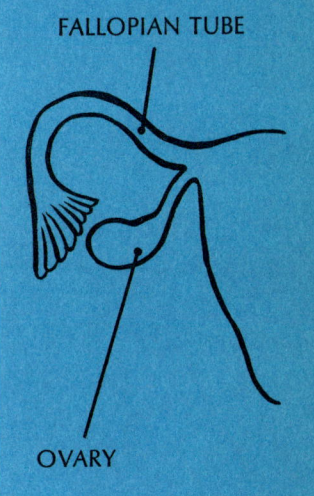

FALLOPIAN TUBE

OVARY

unite with the 23 chromosomes of the mature sperm, resulting in the 46 chromosomes necessary to begin the life of a new human being.

Of the thousands of undeveloped eggs present in the ovaries at the time of a girl's birth, only about 400 are released during her life.

See also: **meiosis, menstruation, multiple birth, ovaries**

ovum An ovum (plural: ova), from the Latin word meaning "egg," is the female reproductive cell. Its function is to join with a male sperm cell to begin the life of a new individual. A mature egg cell, or ovum, is smaller than the period at the end of this sentence, but it contains a nucleus, cytoplasm, cell wall (membrane), and a small amount of yolk.

See also: **fertilization, multiple birth, ovaries, ovulation, sperm**

parturition, see **birth, labor**

paternal Paternal refers to characteristics associated with fathers. It describes terms related to a father. The paternal side of the family means the father's parents, brothers and sisters, aunts and uncles and cousins. Paternal duties are the obligations a father has to his children, such as providing financial support.

See also: **maternal**

paternity Paternity is the state of being a father. One sometimes hears of a "paternity suit," which is not the opposite of a maternity dress. A paternity suit is legal action brought to establish who is the father of a particular child when there is doubt.

See also: **maternity**

pediatrician A pediatrician is a medical doctor who specializes in the care of infants and children. A pediatrician may also care for adolescents and young adults up to the age of 21.

pelvis The pelvis, or pelvic girdle, is the strong ring of bones in the lower part of the body trunk. Bones of the pelvis include the hip bones, bones of the lower end of the spinal column (in back), and a bony plate called the *pubic symphysis* (in front). These bones are tightly connected to one another, forming a basin or cavity which shelters the internal reproductive organs and other organs such as the bladder and rectum.

The shape and size of the pelvic girdle differs considerably between a mature male and female. In the male, the cavity is deeper, more narrow, and funnel-shaped. In the female, the hip bones are wider apart and the cavity is wider, shorter, and straighter at the sides. This larger cavity enables a woman's body to accommodate the size of the expanding uterus during pregnancy. In the final stages of pregnancy, the joints connecting a woman's pelvic bones loosen and separate slightly, making childbirth easier.

penis The penis is the male organ for urination and copulation (sexual intercourse). It is an external organ, tubelike in shape, covered with loose skin. The penis is directly in front of the scrotum, which is between the thighs.

Inside the penis is the urethra, a tiny tube leading from inside the male's body to the outside. The urethra enables urine to pass from the bladder through the penis during urination. After puberty, it also enables semen to pass through the penis during ejaculation.

Surrounding the urethra is a wall of spongelike tissue with many tiny spaces. Normally these spaces are empty, and the penis is soft or limp. When the male is sexually stimulated, blood rushes into these spaces and fills them. The extra blood causes the penis to become firm and enlarged and to stand out from the body. This is called an *erection*. An erection enables the male to insert his penis into the female's vagina during intercourse.

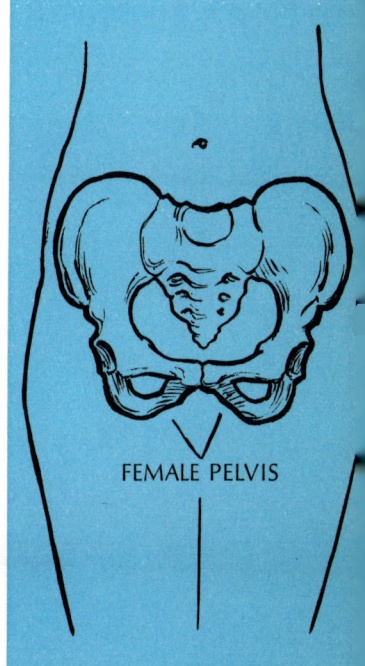

FEMALE PELVIS

The size of the penis varies considerably from one adult male to another. Despite the fact that it might seem the size of a boy's or man's body would indicate the size of his penis, there is little relationship between body size and penis size. Nor is there any relationship between penis size and sexual capability.

The term *phallus*, from the Greek word for penis, is sometimes used to describe something that resembles the male sex organ. A *phallic symbol* is something which reminds people of the penis or of its important part in the reproductive process. Phallic symbols were frequently worshipped in ancient times as part of fertility rites.

See also: **ejaculation, erection, sex hormones, sexual intercourse, urethra**

period, see **menstruation**

petting Petting is the caressing or stroking of the erotic body parts, primarily the breasts and the genitals. Its purpose is sexual arousal. Petting is also called *sexual foreplay* because it helps to make the body ready for sexual intercourse whether or not intercourse is going to be the result.

See also: Book 3, Chapter 20, *Necking, Petting, and Sexual Feelings*

phallic symbol, see **penis**

pill, see **contraception**

pituitary gland Often called the "master gland" of the body, the pituitary is a tiny, rounded gland attached to the base of the brain. Although as small as the tip of the little finger, it controls growth, reproduction, and metabolism.

Acting as the body's "master controller," the pituitary sends out hormones to all of the other glands of the body, stimulating them to perform their specific functions. Some of the glands activated by specific pituitary hormones are the thyroid, adrenals, and gonads (testicles and ovaries).

The pituitary also makes a *growth hormone* in great quantities from the time of birth until adolescent growth has ended. This hormone causes cell growth throughout the body. The effect of the growth hormone and other pituitary hormones is most noticeable around puberty, when bones, muscles, and reproductive organs change most rapidly in size, appearance, and function.

Since all body processes are in some way influenced by the pituitary, any failure of the gland has a noted effect. For example, if the pituitary fails to send out enough growth hormone, a person may be a dwarf. If sex hormones are not sent to the adrenals or gonads, normal reproductive processes and secondary sex characteristics will not develop. Fortunately, it is now possible for doctors to give synthetic (artificial) hormones to make up for those not produced by the pituitary gland.

See also: **hormones, sex hormones**

placenta The placenta is a mass of blood vessels and tissues attached to the wall of the uterus during pregnancy. It is a special organ which enables a developing baby to get nourishment from its mother and to eliminate waste matter.

The placenta is flat, and has a spongy, cakelike appearance when it is completely formed. It is formed when blood vessels and tissues from the embryo combine with blood vessels and tissues from the mother. The two blood systems are close together, but they do not mix. They are separated by a thin wall of cells which allow substances to pass from one blood system to the other.

Blood from the baby travels through the umbilical cord to the placenta and back to the baby again. While it passes through tissues in the placenta, it picks up nourishment, oxygen, and water from the mother's blood vessels and carries them to the baby. Blood also takes harmful carbon dioxide and

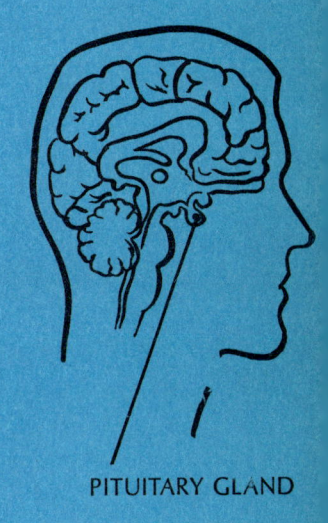

PITUITARY GLAND

PLACENTA

UMBILICAL CORD

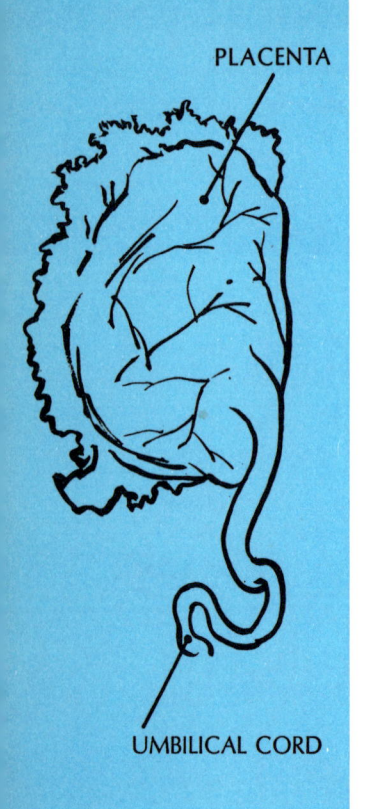

waste matter from the baby's body and leaves it in the placenta. There, it is absorbed by the mother's blood vessels and is discarded through the mother's body.

In addition to serving as an important transfer area between the baby and mother, the placenta also serves as a barrier. It protects the baby from most harmful disease, infections, or drugs which might be in the mother's body. However, it is not a complete barrier. It cannot keep some disease-causing viruses and some drugs from reaching the baby, so a mother must guard her health. The placenta also sends out hormones which are important to the baby's development and birth.

After the baby is born, the placenta is expelled from the uterus along with the portion of the umbilical cord remaining after the cord is cut and the amniotic tissues. This is called the *afterbirth*.

See also: **amnion, labor, navel, umbilical cord**

planned parenthood, see **contraception, family planning**

platonic love The name of the Greek philosopher Plato is given to the form of close friendship called platonic love. Plato believed that love was the basis of a series of steps that progressed from sexual love for one individual to nonsexual love for all people, then to love for laws and ideas, and finally to the contemplation and knowledge of universal truth and beauty.

In popular usage, platonic love means a close relationship between two people, of the same or opposite sex, in which sexual desire does not play a part.

polygamy, see **monogamy**

pornography Pornography is any material (such as a book or movie) whose only purpose is to arouse a person sexually. The word comes from a Greek word meaning "the writing of prostitutes." There are popular phrases that have been applied to pornography. It has been called any "depiction or representation of sexual behavior" which appeals only to a person's "prurient interests" and has no "redeeming social value."

Attitudes about pornography are always changing. What is called pornographic at one time may no longer be thought so at another time. For instance, much of the literature studied in colleges today was once considered pornographic.

Governments have frequently tried to control the buying and selling of pornographic materials, and to insure that they would be kept away from children. Enforcing such laws is always difficult because people disagree over the meaning of pornography. What some people consider pornographic may not seem so to others. Very often a dispute about what is or is not pornographic has to be settled in court. A judge then decides whether or not a certain material is pornographic, and if it should be made available to the public.

See also: **obscenity**

potency Potency is a term that is usually used to refer to the ability of a male to have an erection for sexual intercourse. The opposite is impotence.

See also: **erection, impotence, virility**

pregnancy Pregnancy is the condition of a female who has a developing baby in her uterus. Pregnancy lasts from fertilization to birth of the baby.

With one exception, pregnancy can come about only as a result of sexual intercourse between a female and a male. That one exception is pregnancy resulting from artificial insemination, which is occasionally used with humans. Only when there is a fertile egg present to join with a sperm can pregnancy take place. If an egg and a sperm do meet, fertilization occurs and pregnancy begins.

Most women cannot tell when they first become

pregnant. A woman may notice a few symptoms, but these signs do not always indicate pregnancy. She may suspect that she is pregnant if she misses a menstrual period. (The uterus will not shed its lining if it has received a fertilized egg.) A tender swelling in her breasts may be caused by the new activity of her mamary glands getting ready to make milk for her baby. A woman may feel tired and nauseous early in pregnancy.

A woman can have a test to find out if she is pregnant. Some *pregnancy tests* involve the injection of her urine into a laboratory test animal, such as a frog, mouse, or rabbit. If the woman is pregnant, her urine will contain hormones which activate the ovaries of the test animal. There are other recently developed tests that do not require the use of animals. All these tests can detect pregnancy in its early stages — usually within two weeks after the first missed period.

A doctor can examine a woman to determine if she is pregnant. In a pelvic examination he can note a change in the color of vaginal tissues as well as a new softness of the uterus. In later stages of pregnancy a doctor can hear the fetal heartbeat through a stethoscope.

When a physician determines that a woman is pregnant, he will figure out approximately when her baby will be born. The term of human pregnancy usually lasts about 280 days from the time of the woman's last menstrual period. The baby's birth can come earlier or later than expected.

Pregnancy is a happy time for most women. If an expectant mother is careful about her diet, rest, and exercise, she should feel and look well. The normal weight gain for a pregnant woman is about 20 to 25 pounds. Much of this gain is accounted for by the weight of the baby itself, the placenta, the amniotic fluid and membranes, the swollen uterus, and the increased amount of blood and breast size.

Pregnancy can be divided into three "trimesters" of three months each. In the first trimester all of the vital organs of the embryo are formed. The mother may feel morning sickness and fatigue during this period. In the second trimester the woman's uterus swells to accommodate the growing fetus. She will start to feel the *signs of life* — the movements of her baby within her womb. During the third trimester both the mother and baby will gain weight. A woman may feel awkward because of her large, swollen abdomen. Her baby will probably be constantly active, and his occasional kicks will tell her that he is almost ready to be born.

The end of pregnancy is the birth of a baby.

See also: **amnion, birth, embryo, fertilization, labor, morning sickness, prenatal care, uterus;** Book 2, Chapter 9, *How a Baby Develops;* Book 2, Chapter 10, *The Mother of the Baby*

premarital, see **marital**

premature birth A birth is considered premature when the newborn baby weighs less than $5^1/_2$ pounds. Usually, a premature baby is born two or more weeks earlier than the normal full-term time of nine months. (The normal weight for full-term babies varies from $5^1/_2$ to 11 pounds; the average is seven pounds.)

Since premature babies have not had enough time to develop completely inside their mother's uterus, they require special care, including the controlled environment of an incubator. With this care, many premature babies are able to live. The closer the baby is to being full-term, the better are his chances for survival.

See also: **full-term baby, incubator**

prenatal care Prenatal care is the care and attention given to a woman during her pregnancy. A woman should maintain her health during pregnancy to insure the best possible development of her child.

It is wise for a woman to see her doctor about once a month while she is pregnant. When the time nears for her baby to be born, the doctor will ask to see her more often. During these visits her doctor will check such things as her blood pressure and urine. He can learn a great deal about the baby's development from these checks. Also, he will measure the organs which will be involved when she gives birth. He wants to make sure that they will be able to accommodate a full-grown baby during the birth process. A doctor also tests the blood of a pregnant woman and of her husband, in order to determine if there is any chance of Rh incompatibility between the baby and the mother. If so, the doctor will be prepared to give the baby a blood transfusion should he need it.

The most important advice a doctor gives to a pregnant woman usually concerns her diet. Her unborn baby gets his food supply through the placenta which is connected to his mother. Whatever she eats will determine his diet.

Pregnant women should get plenty of rest. Becoming overtired will make pregnancy and, possibly, delivery more difficult. Adequate exercise is important for all expectant mothers, and a daily walk outdoors is excellent for their health.

A sudden change in life style is not necessary when a woman becomes pregnant. Pregnancy is a perfectly normal condition. Any healthy woman should be able to care for herself as she ordinarily would and still provide her unborn baby with all he needs to grow into a healthy child.

See also: **obstetrician, pregnancy, Rh factor;** Book 2, Chapter 10, *The Mother of the Baby*

primary sex characteristics, see **reproductive organs**

progesterone, see **sex hormones**

promiscuous A promiscuous person is a male or female who has sexual intercourse with a great many people.

prophylactic Prophylactic comes from the Greek word meaning "to keep guard before." In present usage it means to guard against or prevent disease. It is most often used to mean a device for preventing venereal infection. This device, usually called a *condom,* is a thin covering, usually rubber, worn over the penis during sexual intercourse. It is also used as a means of contraception.

See also: **contraception, venereal disease**

prostate The prostate is a partly glandular, partly muscular organ located around the base of the male's urethra. The glandular part secretes fluid which mixes with sperm and other fluids to form semen. Semen helps to keep the sperm alive. The muscular part of the prostate helps to force semen out through the urethra during ejaculation.

See also: **semen, urethra**

prostitute A prostitute is usually a woman who has sexual relations for money. There are also male prostitutes whose sex partners are usually homosexuals.

protoplasm Protoplasm is the jellylike mass in a living cell. It contains the nucleus, cytoplasm, mitochondria, Golgi bodies, and all other parts of the cell. Protoplasm is enclosed by the cell membrane and is thought to consist of protein, other organic and inorganic substances, and water. It is regarded as basic living matter.

See also: **cell**

puberty Puberty is the age at which a boy or girl is first able to reproduce. For reproduction to be possible, a girl's ovaries must release ova (eggs) and a boy's testicles must produce sufficient healthy sperm to fertilize an ovum.

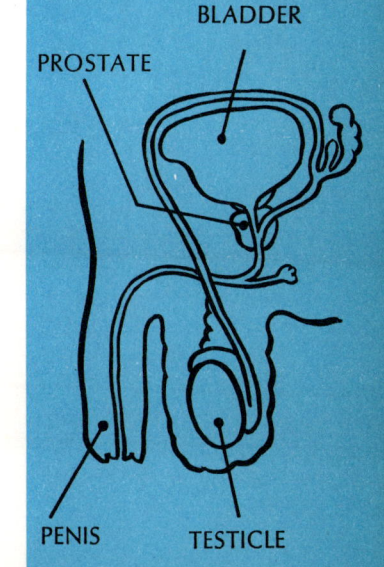

The most dramatic sign that a girl has reached puberty is her first menstruation, although she may not actually be able to reproduce until several months later. For a boy, the sign is first ejaculation.

Prior to puberty, reproductive organs begin to grow and secondary sex characteristics start to appear. It is not abnormal, however, for some of these changes to take place after puberty.

The usual sequence of changes leading to puberty for a girl is: beginning breast development, appearance of pubic hair, menstruation. The usual sequence for a boy is: beginning growth of the scrotum and testes, appearance of pubic hair, lengthening and enlargement of the penis, early voice change, ejaculation.

Although the average age for reaching puberty in the United States is $12^{1}/_{2}$ for girls and $13^{1}/_{2}$ for boys, these ages can vary greatly. It is normal for a boy or girl to reach puberty anywhere between 9 and 17 years of age.

Heredity is one factor that determines when puberty will occur. Environmental factors such as nutrition, disease, or emotional conditions may also affect the time of puberty.

See also: **adolescence, ejaculation, menstruation;** Book 1, Chapter 3, *A Boy Becomes a Man;* Book 1, Chapter 4, *A Girl Becomes a Woman*

pubic hair Pubic hair is short, curly hair that grows in the external genital area. (*Pubes* is Latin for "hair.") Its appearance is one of the first signs of the approach of puberty.

See also: **puberty**

quadruplets, see **multiple birth**

quintuplets, see **multiple birth**

rape Rape is sexual intercourse forced on an unconsenting person. Usually, it is an attack by a man upon a woman. It is a crime, and the penalties are quite severe. Some states fix the maximum penalty at life imprisonment or execution.

Statutory rape is a legal term meaning sexual intercourse with a female who is a minor, whether or not she gives her consent.

See also: **seduction**

reproduction Reproduction is the process by which all living things produce offspring. The process may be either *asexual* (without sex) or *sexual*.

Asexual reproduction requires only a single parent which is sometimes referred to as the mother, although it is neither female nor male. There are three types of asexual reproduction: division, budding, and spores. These forms of reproduction are common only among the most primitive types of plants and animals. Some of these life forms are also capable of sexual reproduction.

Sexual reproduction requires the participation of a male and a female parent. It is the way most plants and animals, including human beings, provide for the continuation of their own kind. The male parent produces cells called spermatozoa, or sperm, and the female parent produces ova, or egg cells. The two kinds of cells join in the act of fertilization, and a new organism begins to develop. After a period of development, the length of which depends upon the particular species, a new being will exist. This plant or animal will mature and will one day be capable of reproduction, thus assuring the continuation of its species.

See also: **asexual, fertilization, life cycle**; Book 1, Chapter 1, *The Life Cycle*; Book 2, Chapter 9, *How a Baby Develops*

reproductive organs The reproductive organs are the sex organs which make reproduction possible. They are also known as the genitals, or genitalia.

The external (outside) genitals of the human male are the penis and scrotum. The scrotum contains the testicles, or testes. The male's internal (inside) sex organs are the vas deferens, seminal vesicles, ejaculatory ducts, spermatic cords, prostate, and Cowper's gland.

The external genitals of the human female are

the vulva: labia majora, labia minora, mons veneris, and clitoris. Her internal sex organs are the ovaries, uterus, vagina, and Fallopian tubes.

See also: **clitoris, epididymis, Fallopian tubes, labia, ovaries, penis, prostate, scrotum, seminal vesicles, testicles, uterus, vagina, vas deferens**

Rh factor The Rh factor is a substance found in the red blood cells of about 86 percent of human beings. A person with this substance is said to be *Rh positive (Rh+)*, and a person without it is *Rh negative (Rh−)*. The Rh factor receives its name from the Rhesus monkey, which also has this substance in its blood.

The Rh factor is important in pregnancy. When an Rh− mother conceives a child with an Rh+ father, the developing baby may have the father's Rh+ factor. If some of the baby's Rh+ blood passes through the placenta into the mother's blood, the mother's body builds antibodies against it. If too much of this antibody passes back from the mother to the placenta, it may destroy the baby's red blood cells, resulting in what is called a "blue baby."

Because of advances in medical science, the problem of an Rh conflict is not as serious as it once was. Today, doctors test the blood of an Rh− woman during each pregnancy to determine the effect of antibodies on her baby's blood. With special care, the diseases or deaths caused by antibodies have been greatly reduced in number.

See also: **prenatal care**

rhythm method, see **contraception**

romance A romance is an emotional, enchanting affair. A romance can be in the form of a story which tells about exciting, heroic adventures. Romantic music is stirring music that appeals to people's emotions.

A love affair is often called a romance. Romantic

love is thought to be impulsive, blindly emotional love. A person involved in a romance sees in his loved one only those qualities that he wants to see. He loves idealistically and does not consider his loved one's faults.

Romantic love can be an exciting, thrilling adventure, but it is sometimes temporary, and it dissolves when the mystery and adventure of the affair disappear. Although romantic love is not thought to be strong and lasting, romance always plays a part in love between men and women.

See also: **crush, infatuation, love;** Book 3, Chapter 22, *How Do You Know When It's Love*

rubber, see **contraception, prophylactic**

rupture, see **hernia**

sadism Sadism refers to the attainment of sexual pleasure through inflicting cruelty upon one's partner. The word comes from the name of a French novelist, the Marquis de Sade, who both practiced and wrote about the abnormality.

See also: **masochism**

sanitary belt, see **menstruation**

sanitary pad, see **menstruation**

scrotum The scrotum is the sac of skin in male mammals that contains the testicles. In men it is located between the thighs, directly behind the penis. The scrotum is divided internally into two compartments, each containing one testicle.

Normally, the testicles descend from the abdominal cavity into the scrotal pouch during the seventh month of fetal development. In about 2 percent of male babies, one or both testicles may not descend by the time of birth, and in about 7 percent of this group, they may remain undescended at puberty. It is the general opinion of physicians that an undescended testicle should be dealt with by the time a boy is six years old.

Because the scrotum is outside the body, the testicles are kept at a temperature slightly lower than normal body temperature. This lower temperature is necessary for the production of sperm.

See also: **semen, sperm, testicles**

secondary sex characteristics Secondary sex characteristics are the physical features other than the external sex organs which cause the male and female to differ in outward appearance. These characteristics differ from *primary sex characteristics* in that they are not necessary for reproduction.

Beginning at puberty, hormones from the testes of the male and from the ovaries of the female stimulate the appearance and growth of secondary sex characteristics.

In girls, secondary sex characteristics include the development of breasts, an increase of fat on the hips and thighs, and the growth of pubic hair around the genital area.

In boys, secondary sex characteristics include a deeper voice pitch and the growth of hair on the face, at the base of the penis, and usually on the chest. Also considered a secondary sex characteristic of boys is a body build which is usually more muscular and larger than that of a girl.

See also: **puberty, sex hormones**

seduction Seduction is the act of inducing someone to engage in sexual intercourse. It is different from rape in that force is not used by the seducer. Seduction is accomplished by means of flattery, gifts, or erotic stimulation.

See also: **rape**

semen Semen, from the Latin word for "seed," is the thick, whitish fluid ejaculated from the penis at the time of orgasm. Also called *seminal fluid,* it is a mixture of sperm and liquids necessary for the fertilization of the egg.

Sperm is produced in the testicles, travels through the vas deferens, and is stored in the epididymis. Both the prostate and the seminal vesicles secrete liquids which mix with the sperm to form semen. These liquids enable the sperm to swim and to survive the slightly acid conditions of the male urethra and of the vagina.

See also: **ejaculation, sperm, testicles**

seminal emission A seminal emission is an ejaculation of semen which generally occurs at night during sleep. For this reason, a seminal emission is also called a *nocturnal emission* or a *wet dream*. It may or may not be accompanied by dreams.

Although adult men may also have seminal emissions, they are most common during the adolescent years. It is a normal way that the body rids itself of excess sperm, which are produced constantly in the sexually mature male.

See also: Book 1, Chapter 3, *A Boy Becomes a Man*

seminal vesicles The seminal vesicles are two small pouches in a male which are located at the back of the prostate gland. After sperm leaves the vas deferens, it flows into the seminal vesicles where it is stored. The seminal vesicles lead into the urethra through which sperm flows.

See also: **prostate, semen, sperm**

sensual Sensual means having to do with the senses. It refers specifically to satisfying appetites, or the attainment of sexual pleasure through the senses. Sensual can also mean excessive devotion to indulgence of the body to the neglect of spiritual or intellectual interests.

sensuous This word is often confused with *sensual*. While both words relate to the five senses of sight, smell, hearing, taste, and touch, sensuous means primarily delight in a form of beauty that is gratifying to one sense. For example, a person can experience sensuous enjoyment of a painting, which appeals to his sense of sight; a perfume, which appeals to his smell; a symphony, which appeals to his hearing; a strawberry, which appeals to his taste, or a luxurious fur coat, which appeals to his sense of touch.

sex The word *sex*, used in many different ways, refers to the basic differences between male and female plants, animals, and humans. Being of either male or female sex means having the physical appearances, reproductive functions, and behavior common to that particular sex.

Sex also refers to the inborn instinct that causes males and females to reproduce. This is the natural attraction of one sex for the other that enables the life cycle to continue. Sex is basic to all the higher forms of animal life. Its expression in the sex act is natural and right.

See also: **femininity, masculinity, sex determination, sexuality**

sex abnormalities, see **deviation, hermaphrodite**

sex appeal Sex appeal is the personal attraction individual members of one sex have for individual members of the other. While sex appeal is frequently thought of as being a physical quality, it is really made up of many different aspects of a total personality. Everybody has sex appeal for somebody — the discovery of this truth is one of the delights and mysteries of human nature.

See also: **heterosexuality, sexuality**

sex determination The sex of a child is fixed, or determined, by a chromosome from the male sperm cell at the instant of conception.

Each ovum and sperm cell contains 23 chromosomes. One of the 23 chromosomes is a *sex chromosome*. In a female the sex chromosome is always female. The female chromosome is labeled "X". In the male the sex chromosome of the sperm can be male or female. A sperm has an "X" female chromosome or a "Y" male chromosome.

The sperm and ovum join and begin a new life. If the sperm carries a "Y" sex chromosome, the child will have an "XY" combination and will be a boy. If the sperm carries an "X" sex chromosome, the child will have an "XX" combination, and will be a girl.

See also: **chromosome, conceive**

sex drive The sex drive is the desire for sexual expression and satisfaction found in all animals, including human beings. It is what makes them want to mate; therefore, it assures the continuation of the life cycle. If the sex drive were not a natural part of life, life itself would cease to exist.

In human beings, of course, sexual desire becomes much more complex than it is among the lower animals. It is not only physical, but is very much affected by such things as learned attitudes, experiences, customs, ideals, and environment. Among people, the satisfaction of sexual desire is subject to the sanctions of society.

See also: Book 1, Chapter 1, *The Life Cycle*; Book 3, Chapter 20, *Necking, Petting, and Sexual Feelings*

sex education Any instruction that is designed to acquaint young people with the facts of human reproduction and the roles they are supposed to play in the process can be called sex education.

Teaching can be as formal as conducting family living classes in school with the newest audiovisual aids, or as informal as watching the family cat give birth to kittens. Traditionally, father-son and mother-daughter talks concerning "the birds and bees" or "the facts of life" have been supposed to take place when children reached puberty. In reality, children in many cases pass on to each other, generation after generation, distorted "facts" frequently disguised as "dirty jokes."

Although boys and girls have been learning

EGG CELL   SPERM CELL
   X   X
       ↓   ↓
       XX
   FERTILIZED EGG
         ↓
       GIRL

   X   Y
       ↓   ↓
       XY
   FERTILIZED EGG
         ↓
       BOY

SEX DETERMINATION

about sex in one way or another for thousands of years, when people in the United States today speak of "sex education" they are usually referring to a fairly recent phenomenon. Instruction in family living and the biology of human reproduction is still not nationwide.

Those who support the idea of sex education in the public schools hope to help all young people to understand human sexuality as part of healthy living and to give adolescents facts instead of fantasies about sex. People who oppose the idea usually cite the diversity of social practice, religious belief, and private opinion about sexual matters in this country as factors arguing against public school instruction in these matters.

sex hormones Sex hormones are chemical substances in the body which control all sexual (reproductive) characteristics, growth, and functions of an individual. There are many different sex hormones and they all work together, each playing a necessary part in the life cycle of both the male and the female.

Male sex hormones are called *androgens*. Among those things they are responsible for are secondary sex characteristics—the growth of facial and pubic hair and deeper voice pitch. Androgens also influence the sex drive in men and women.

Female sex hormones are called *estrogens*. They influence the development of secondary sex characteristics in girls—breast development, feminine body shape, and the appearance of body hair. They also play a large part in regulating the menstrual cycle.

Androgens and estrogens are both present in the male and female. Their action is still not completely understood, but physicians are aware of their importance and of the necessity of maintaining proper balance between them in each sex. If nature has erred in the distribution of male or female sex hormones, a doctor can administer pills or injections to restore the balance.

See also: **androgens, estrogens, hormones, pituitary gland, secondary sex characteristics;** Book 1, Chapter 3, *A Boy Becomes a Man;* Book 1, Chapter 4, *A Girl Becomes a Woman*

sexual   Sexual is a word used to describe actions or conditions associated with sex. Sexual reproduction is the continuation of the life cycle through the union of a male and female of the same species. This differs from the *asexual reproduction* of some lower life forms, which reproduce without the union of two sexes.

sexual intercourse   Sexual intercourse is the intimate physical union of a man and a woman. This is the reproductive act of human beings that enables the sperm and egg to unite to begin the life of a new individual. Other terms used to describe this act are *coitus* (from the Latin for *uniting*) and *copulation* (meaning *binding together*).

Before a man and woman have sexual intercourse they usually kiss and caress each other. This sexual stimulation causes the man's penis to become erect so that it may be inserted into the vagina. It also causes the woman's vagina to be moist and relaxed, in order to receive the penis.

The act of intercourse begins when the penis is inserted into the vagina. During intercourse, the partner's bodies move in a rhythmic way, causing a gentle friction between the penis and vaginal walls. When stimulation reaches a pleasurable peak, or climax, orgasm occurs. In the male, orgasm is accompanied by the ejaculation of semen (containing the sperm) from the penis. In the female, orgasm occurs when muscles of the vagina and uterus contract strongly.

Sperm, deposited in the upper part of the vagina during ejaculation, travel through the uterus to the Fallopian tubes. If a sperm meets with and joins an egg in the Fallopian tube, fertilization occurs. Fertilization does not occur every time a man and woman have sexual intercourse.

Since sexual intercourse is the most intimate expression of love between a man and a woman, the act is sometimes called *making love*. People who have this close, intimate relationship are said to have *sexual relations* with each other.

See also: Book 2, Chapter 8, *The Beginning of a Life Cycle;* Book 3, Chapter 20, *Necking, Petting, and Sexual Feelings*

sexuality Sexuality is the total functioning of an individual as a male or female human being. It is responsiveness to every act and fact of living with other people according to the nature of one's own established and accepted manhood or womanhood. Sexuality involves the recognition by both men and women of the life force within them, and of their actual or potential part in the life cycle. If life is for living and loving and learning—and it is—then sexuality is to celebrate life.

shaving Shaving is the removal of facial or body hair with the use of a razor or electric shaver. Originally, shaving applied only to the removal of hair from a boy's or man's face. In the United States today, it is also common for girls and women to shave the hair from their legs and under their arms.

Beginning at puberty, a boy's face begins to have a growth of light-colored, fine hair sometimes called "peach fuzz." In time, as this hair becomes darker and thicker, it is commonly referred to as "whiskers." Usually a boy shaves occasionally as the fuzz first appears and gradually works up to shaving once or twice a day, depending upon the heaviness or darkness of his beard. Facial hair growth of a boy or man who shaves only partially or not at all develops into *sideburns* (on the side of the cheek), a *beard* (on the chin and cheek), and a *mustache* (on the upper lip).

See also: Book 1, Chapter 3, *A Boy Becomes a Man*

Siamese twins Siamese twins are identical twins who are joined at one part of their bodies. This extremely rare type of twinning occurs if the fertilized egg begins dividing as for identical twins, but does not separate completely into two new cells. The twins will be joined by the bridge of body tissue at the point where the cells failed to separate.

See also: **multiple birth**

sibling A sibling is one of two or more persons who are offspring of the same parents. If you have a brother, he is your sibling. If you have a sister, she is also your sibling. The word comes from an old English word *sib*, meaning "related by blood."

skin disturbances, see **acne**

smoking Smoking is the act of inhaling and exhaling tobacco smoke, especially that of cigarettes. It also includes pipe and cigar smoking. Today, it is generally agreed that cigarette smoking can be harmful, especially for those who smoke a pack or more a day for an extended length of time.

A principal component of tobacco smoke is *nicotine,* an oily drug that turns brown when exposed to air. It works on the nerves and muscles of the body, at first stimulating and then depressing them. It can also act on the circulatory system, at first slowing the rate of the heartbeat and later causing it to become faster than usual. In concentrated form, nicotine is poisonous. Although a cigarette contains much less than a lethal (killing) dose of nicotine, some *is* absorbed by smoking.

In the 1930s, surgeons and health officials first became aware of the great increase in lung cancer in the United States, particularly in men. (Not many women smoked in the '30s.) According to the Public Affairs Committee, 371 deaths due to lung cancer were reported in 1914. By 1930, the number had risen to 2,357. It seemed evident, in studies in the 1940s and 1950s, that the increase in cigarette smoking was the major cause of increased death due to lung cancer. The disease can occur in non-smokers, but in countries where few people smoke, it is rare.

By 1964, the number of deaths due to lung cancer had risen to 43,000 per year. In that year the Report of the Surgeon General's Advisory Committee on Smoking and Health presented the most serious warning to date on the dangers of smoking. Some of the chief findings are that: 1) Cigarette smoking is a definite health hazard which demands appropriate action in the United States; 2) There is a definite relationship between cigarette smoking and lung cancer in men. (Data on women seems to indicate the same relationship.); 3) Cigarette smoking is a significant cause of cancer of the larynx (the voice organ); 4) Chances of developing lung cancer increase with the number of cigarettes smoked per day and the number of years a person continues to smoke. These chances are lessened if a person stops smoking immediately.

Other damage to the heart, lungs, and other body parts has also been linked to smoking. The most significant evidence of the danger of smoking is that non-smokers generally live considerably longer than smokers.

More and more people consider the seriousness of smoking and stop. Others continue, however, because cigarette smoking is a very strong habit. Since the habit is so difficult to break, the best way to avoid the hazards of smoking is never to start.

social diseases, see **venereal disease**

sodomy Sodomy is derived from the name of the city of Sodom, mentioned in the Bible for the wickedness of its inhabitants. The term today has various meanings both in general usage and according to law. It can mean homosexual intercourse, intercourse with an animal, or some forms of heterosexual intercourse.

sophistication Sophistication is the opposite of simplicity. A simple person could also be described as innocent, uncomplicated, and natural. One who is sophisticated is experienced, complex, and subtle. Sophistication implies an awareness of the ways of the world and an understanding of the many different kinds of people who live in it. Someone has said that the truly sophisticated person is interested in everything but amazed by nothing.

Sometimes young people, in an effort to pretend to knowledge they have not lived long enough to acquire, assume an air of world-weariness or knowing-it-all. Girls may copy the dress and behavior of famous actresses. Boys may boast of their sexual conquests (actual or otherwise). Such pseudo-sophistication, as it is called, is part of growing up and wanting to be an adult. Real sophistication cannot be practiced or purchased or put on. It is an aspect of the personality of the man or woman who is well acquainted with the world, and is acquired by certain people early, by others later, and by some never.

sperm A sperm (or spermatozoon), from the Greek *sperma* meaning "seed," is the male reproductive cell. Its function is to join with a female egg cell (ovum) to begin the life of a new individual.

Each mature human sperm has an oval head, which contains the nucleus, and a long, thin tail which is used to move the entire cell. Sperm are so tiny that a single one must move 500 times its own length in order to travel one inch.

From the time of puberty, sperm are constantly produced in great numbers by the testicles of the sexually mature male in a process called *spermatogenesis*. When they begin maturing in the testicles, sperm cells divide by meiosis, reducing their chromosome number to 23.

From the testicles, sperm are moved by tiny, hairlike *cilia* to the epididymis where they become completely mature. They are stored in the epididymis for a time and are then moved by cilia into the vas deferens.

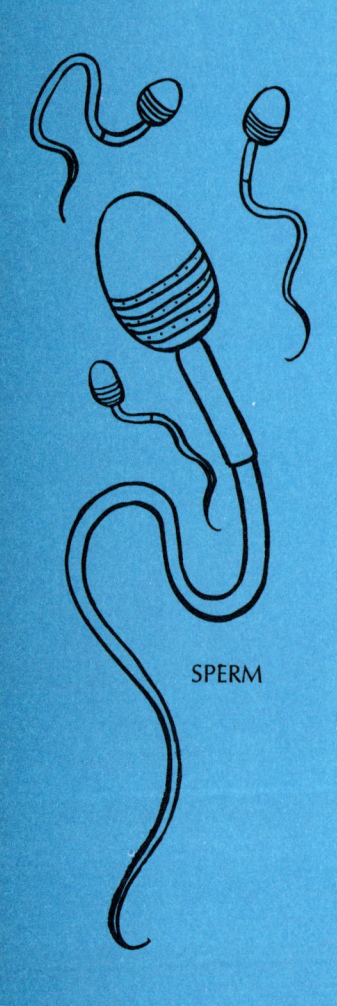

When the male is stimulated sexually, the prostate and seminal vesicles secrete fluids which mix with the sperm to form *semen*. In semen, the sperm immediately become activated and begin to move by lashing their tiny, whiplike tails back and forth. During ejaculation, semen is moved quickly into the urethra and out through the penis. Estimates of the number of sperm ejaculated at one time range from 200 million to 500 million.

If ejaculation occurs during sexual intercourse, sperm are deposited in the vagina. They then travel up through the uterus to the Fallopian tubes. If the sperm arrive near the time of ovulation, one of the many million will probably unite with the mature egg, and fertilization may occur.

See also: **ejaculation, fertilization, germ cell, ovum, semen, sex determination, testicles**

spotting Spotting is the appearance of blood, usually from the vagina, during pregnancy or at a time of the menstrual cycle other than during the actual menses. It may be of little or no importance, or it may be a warning of some disorder of the reproductive organs. If spotting is more than slight, it should be reported to a physician.

See also: **vaginal discharge**

statutory rape, see **rape**

stepchild A stepchild is a boy or girl who has a parent that is related to him only through marriage. For example, the son of a woman who marries for the second time is a stepchild to the new husband, his stepfather. The boy is called a stepson.

If the new husband has children of his own, the two sets of children are stepbrothers and stepsisters to each other.

sterility Sterility, also called infertility, is an inability to reproduce. It occurs for many different reasons in both humans and animals.

A man is sterile if his testicles do not produce sperm, or if the sperm are too few in number. It is estimated that a man's sperm count should be at least 200 million in a normal ejaculation. If the sperm are somehow prevented from traveling from the testicles to the urethra, sterility would result. If sperm are unhealthy or are not active enough to travel all the way to the Fallopian tubes in the female, this would cause a man's sterility.

A woman is sterile if her ovaries do not produce mature eggs or if eggs are not released in ovulation. Another cause might be blockage of the Fallopian tubes, preventing sperm from entering or the egg from moving into the uterus following fertilization. If a woman's body is not able to provide nourishment for a developing baby, or if she consistently miscarries (aborts) before the end of gestation, she might be considered sterile.

There are many other reasons why a man or a woman may be infertile. If one or both partners in a marriage are sterile but they wish to have children, they can seek medical help. A physician can often find out the cause of sterility and correct it.

See also: **fertility**

sterilization Sterilization is the process of making an individual incapable of reproduction.

In the female, sterilization occurs when the ovaries are removed (oophorectomy) or when the Fallopian tubes are cut and tied (tubal ligation). Sterilization also results when the uterus is removed (hysterectomy).

In the male, sterilization occurs when the testicles are removed (castration) or when the tubes leading from the testicles to the urethra are cut and tied (vasectomy). Vasectomy is not always permanent. In 50 percent of all cases, the tubes can be rejoined and a man made fertile again.

In both sexes, sterilization results in an indi-

HORMONES STIMULATE GROWTH

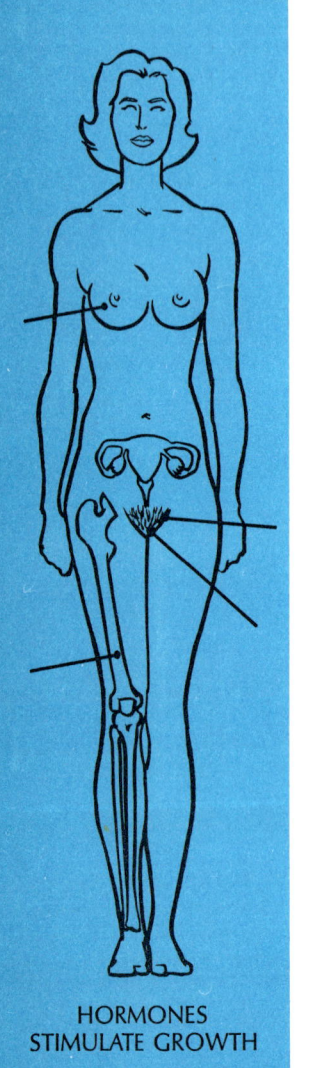

vidual who no longer produces reproductive cells, or whose eggs or sperm cannot function in the reproductive process.

See also: **castration, hysterectomy, reproduction**

stillbirth A stillbirth is the birth of a dead baby after at least 28 weeks of pregnancy. A stillbirth differs from a miscarriage in that the fetus is usually less than 20 weeks old when a miscarriage occurs.

See also: **miscarriage**

stimulation Something that stimulates literally "pushes" something else to act or grow. For example, as children approach the age of puberty, the pituitary gland stimulates the endocrine glands to release hormones. The hormones, in turn, stimulate the growth of the secondary sex characteristics. Boys and girls begin to grow into adolescents, and their new feelings stimulate them to become interested in each other in new ways. All of these little "pushes" are part of the one big "push" with which nature has provided all living things — the urge, or stimulation, to continue their life cycle.

syphilis, see **venereal disease**

tampon, see **menstruation**

teenager, see **adolescence, puberty**

testes, see **testicles**

testicles The testicles, or testes, are the male reproductive glands which produce sperm for fertilization. Testicles also produce the male sex hormone testosterone, which stimulates the growth and maturation of primary and secondary male sex characteristics, such as the growth of the penis, appearance of pubic hair, and lowered voice pitch.

There are two testicles. Each is egglike in shape, about $1^1/_2$ inches long, and about an inch thick.

They are part of the male's external genitals and are contained in a pouch called the scrotum, directly behind the penis. Their location outside the body is necessary because the testicles could not produce sperm in the higher temperature inside the body.

See also: **scrotum, sex hormones, sperm**

thyroid gland The thyroid gland is an endocrine gland located in the neck above the top of the breast bone. Thyroxine is the principle hormone produced by the thyroid gland. Thyroxine works with the pituitary gland and controls bone growth. The thyroid gland also regulates metabolism.

tobacco, see **smoking**

tomboy Tomboy is a name traditionally given to a girl who acts in a carefree, rowdy way more characteristic of boys.

Instead of playing with dolls, reading, and other traditional pursuits among girls, the tomboy enjoys football, baseball, or other vigorous activities.

As attitudes change about what is feminine and proper for girls to do, and they become more active in "boys" activities, the word tomboy will probably drop out of use.

See also: Book 1, Chapter 4, *A Girl Becomes a Woman*

transsexualism Transsexualism is a compulsive desire to become a member of the opposite sex. Sometimes transsexuals have operations performed to make them more like the opposite sex.

transvestite A transvestite is a person who becomes sexually excited from wearing the clothing of the opposite sex. A person can be heterosexual, marry, and have children, and still be a transvestite.

A transvestite seems to desire to become for a

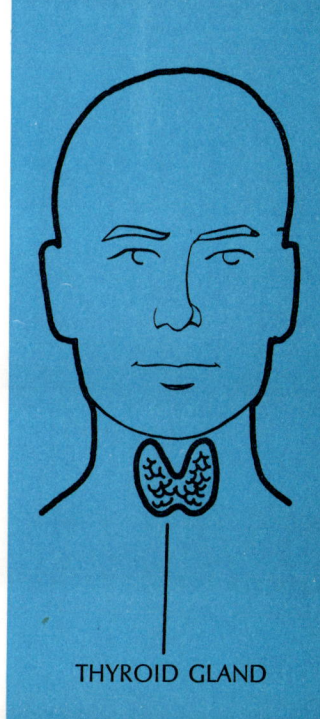

THYROID GLAND

U

while a person of the opposite sex. A male transvestite may even wear the underclothing, shoes, and hosiery of a woman.

triplets, see **multiple birth**

tubal pregnancy, see **Fallopian tubes**

twins, see **multiple birth, Siamese twins**

umbilical cord The umbilical cord is a ropelike structure which connects a developing baby to the placenta. It is attached to the baby's abdomen on one end and to the placenta on the other.

Blood from the baby passes through the umbilical cord to the placenta. There it picks up nourishment and oxygen from the placenta, and brings it to the baby. It also takes waste matter away.

Umbilical cords vary greatly in length. From seven inches to four feet is considered normal. The baby does not usually become tangled in a long cord because blood flowing through the cord moves at a very fast rate and keeps the cord stiff. Also, since the cord is coiled and is always wet, it does not become knotted. It is slippery and can slide around the baby.

After birth, a doctor ties and cuts the umbilical cord near the baby's abdomen. The cutting does not hurt because the cord does not have nerve endings. It does not bleed, either, for a special jelly in the cord closes the blood vessels.

A few weeks after birth, the tied end of the cord dries up and falls off. The indentation remaining in the abdomen is called the navel or, in common terms, the "belly button."

See also: **navel, placenta**

unisex Unisex is a term that came into use in the late 1960s to describe clothing styles which make no distinction between the sexes. The very same pants suits, for example, or ruffled shirts, or jewelry, are sold to males and females. Only the tailoring varies slightly because of the undeniable anatomical differences between men and women.

Some people who study society see unisex as a definite trend for the future, and are displeased or pleased about it, depending on whether they think more or less emphasis should be placed on sexual differences. Others see the desire to dress alike as simply a passing fad that is amusing while it lasts.

See also: **femininity, masculinity, sex**

urethra The urethra is a tube through which urine passes out of the body from the bladder. In the male body, the urethra also serves as a passageway for semen when it is ejaculated.

In the physically mature male, the urethra is from eight to nine inches long. It begins at the bladder, passes close to the prostate, travels through the penis, and opens outside the body at the end of the penis. Near the prostate, there are tiny openings that allow semen to pass into the urethra during ejaculation.

Although both urine and semen pass through the urethra, the two never mix. When semen is ejaculated, a special valve in the bladder keeps urine from passing into the urethra. When urination occurs, another valve keeps semen from passing into the urethra.

In females, the urethra is much shorter (1 to $1^1/_2$ inches long), and is not intermixed in the reproductive system. The outside opening of the urethra is in the vulva, in front of the vaginal opening.

See also: **penis, prostate**

urine Urine is the yellowish liquid containing waste matter, especially that resulting from the digestion of proteins. It is discharged from the body through the urethra. Urine is formed in the kidneys. It passes to the bladder, accumulates there, and is then expelled or voided from the body in the process of *urination*.

See also: **feces**

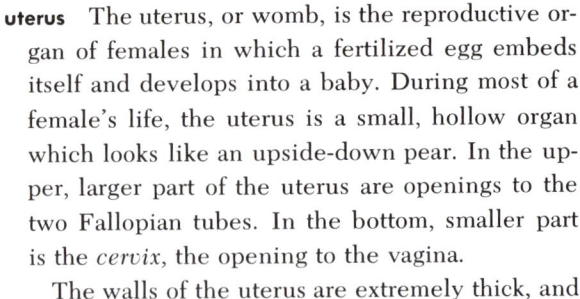

uterus The uterus, or womb, is the reproductive organ of females in which a fertilized egg embeds itself and develops into a baby. During most of a female's life, the uterus is a small, hollow organ which looks like an upside-down pear. In the upper, larger part of the uterus are openings to the two Fallopian tubes. In the bottom, smaller part is the *cervix*, the opening to the vagina.

The walls of the uterus are extremely thick, and contain strong muscle fibers. The inner lining of the uterus is called the *endometrium*. These walls become enriched with blood at a certain time each month. If fertilization of an egg cell does not occur, this blood is discharged from the uterus as the menstrual flow.

If fertilization does occur, the embryo embeds itself into the endometrium and takes nourishment from the rich blood supply in the wall. In time, blood vessels and tissues of the embryo combine with blood vessels and tissues of the uterine wall to form the placenta. The placenta enables the developing baby to take nourishment from the mother's blood and to get rid of waste matter.

During pregnancy, the strong muscles of the uterus expand greatly to give the developing baby room to grow. During birth, these muscles contract forcefully, pushing the baby out of the uterus through the vagina. Following birth, the uterus gradually regains its normal size and shape.

vagina The vagina is the passageway between the internal female reproductive organs and the outside of the body. It is a tube about 4 to 6 inches in length, with muscular walls that are normally in close contact with one another. Internally, the vagina is connected to the cervix, the opening to the uterus. Externally, it opens in the vulva area behind the urethral opening.

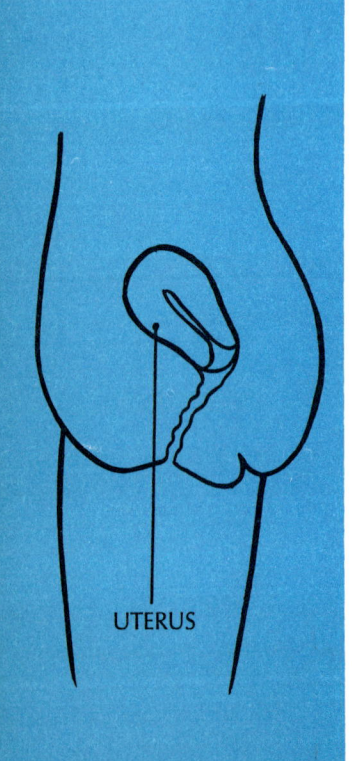

The vagina performs three important functions in the reproductive cycle. 1) It enables menstrual flow to pass from the body. 2) It receives the penis during sexual intercourse. 3) It enables a baby to pass from the uterus to outside of the body during childbirth. For this last reason, the vagina is also called the *birth canal*. During childbirth, it expands greatly to accommodate the size of the baby.

vaginal discharge A vaginal discharge is a fluid secreted from the vagina of sexually mature females. A vaginal discharge can be normal or abnormal, depending upon the amount and the cause.

Doctors use the term *leukorrhea* for vaginal discharge. Leukorrhea, from the Greek words *leukos* and *roia* meaning "white flow," is a whitish, mucous discharge. It is caused by the many tiny bacilli in the vagina, which provide natural immunity to infection or germs during the childbearing years. A slight amount of leukorrhea is normal, especially just before and after menstruation.

When vaginal discharge is excessive or irritating and accompanied by pain or itching, it is usually caused by an infection in the vagina. Proper medical treatment will cure the infection. During pregnancy, leukorrhea and other vaginal discharges are increased, often causing discomfort that can be aided medically. Any unusual discharge at any time should be reported to a physician.

During sexual intercourse or excitement, the vagina may also discharge part of the lubrication that results from sexual stimulation. This is not an ejaculation as in the male, but is a normal discharge of excess moisture.

vas deferens The vas deferens is a long tube or duct that runs from the epididymis to the seminal vesicle. There are two vas deferens in the male body, each leading to one seminal vesicle. Each vas deferens is about 18 inches long and serves as a passageway for sperm. The vas deferens can also be

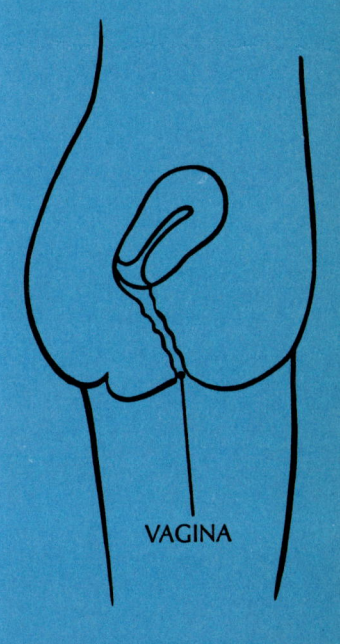

VAGINA

a storage place for sperm, especially at its upper end where it joins the seminal vesicle.

See also: **epididymis, seminal vesicles, sperm**

venereal disease Venereal disease, or VD, is a term given to all diseases which are contracted through sexual intercourse. The most serious venereal diseases, also called *social diseases,* are responsible for physical and mental damage, and death.

The two most common types of VD in the United States are *gonorrhea* and *syphilis.* Their seriousness and the increasing number of cases are of major concern to all public health officials.

Syphilis and gonorrhea are caused by two entirely different germs which attack the body in different ways. Syphilis, caused by a spiral-like germ called a *spirochete,* can cause extreme damage to both the mind and body. Each year in the United States about 4,000 people die of syphilis. In mental hospitals, over $50 million a year is spent to care for patients with syphilitic psychosis.

The first symptoms of syphilis appear quite soon after sexual contact with an infected person. Spirochetes pass into the body through the skin and multiply rapidly, usually on the external sex organs, but also on the lip, nipple of the breast, mouth, urethra, or vagina. Within about three weeks, a painless sore called a *chancre* (pronounced shank' er) appears where the spirochetes entered.

Other signs of syphilis that may occur following infection are: a rash on any part of the body, sore throat, high fever, severe headaches, and a loss of hair causing bald spots.

Although the chancre and other symptoms may disappear within a few months, spirochetes will continue to invade parts of the body if the disease is not cured. They may attack the heart, brain, liver, bones, or other body parts. Eventually, in anywhere from 2 to 25 years, the person with syphilis may become mentally ill, crippled, blind, may develop heart disease, or may even die.

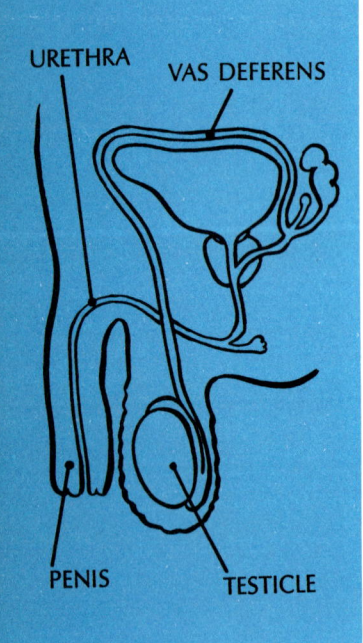

If a woman with syphilis becomes pregnant, her baby may contract *congenital syphilis* and be born dead or deformed. Today, however, laws protect most unborn babies from this disease. Most states require blood tests, which detect syphilis, of men and women before they obtain a marriage license and/or during the early months of pregnancy.

Gonorrhea, caused by tiny bacteria called *gonococci*, is the most common venereal disease. It can cause blindness, sterility, severe arthritis, and damage to the heart and brain. If left untreated, gonorrhea can cause death to those who contact it.

The first symptoms of gonorrhea appear about three to five days following sexual contact with an infected person. In boys and men, the presence of gonococci causes a puslike discharge from the sex organs and an extremely painful, burning feeling during urination. A male will frequently see a physician immediately because of this pain, and the disease will be detected.

Girls or women who contract gonorrhea seldom have these symptoms, and many cases of gonorrhea in the female go undetected until serious harm has been done. Some slight indications of gonorrhea may be a redness and tenderness in the labia and around the vaginal or urethral openings.

If gonorrhea is not cured in its early stages, it may invade the internal reproductive organs of men or women, causing sterility. If gonococci are transferred to the eyes, by contaminated hands or clothes, they can quickly cause blindness. A pregnant woman with gonorrhea may pass the disease to her baby during childbirth, leading to blindness.

Venereal diseases can be avoided through abstinence, and they can be cured if detected during their early stages. People who notice any of the symptoms of VD, or believe they have had contact with an infected person, should immediately see a physician or go to a local public health center. Tests can determine the presence of a specific venereal disease, and drugs (penicillin and other antibiotics) can cure the disease.

vernix The vernix is a kind of protective covering on the skin of the developing fetus. It is formed of sebum from the oil glands and cells shed from the outer layer of skin. The vernix clings to the surface of the unborn infant's skin and keeps it from becoming water-soaked as it floats in the amniotic sac. Babies are usually bathed right after they are born and the vernix is washed away before their mothers see them.

See also: **amnion, oil glands**

virginity Virginity is the state of being a virgin. A virgin is a female or a male who has never had sexual intercourse. The word *virgin* is also sometimes used to mean anything pure and untouched, such as a virgin forest.

See also: **defloration, hymen**

virility Virility refers to manly vigor. It means specifically the ability to function as a male in sexual intercourse.

See also: **masculinity, potency**

voyeurism Voyeurism is a sexual deviation in which a person receives gratification from observing the sexual parts of another person's body or acts of sexual intercourse. The word comes from the French *voyeur,* meaning "one who sees." In its extreme form voyeurism is personified in the "peeping Tom" who makes a habit of spying on other people, especially women who are undressing or undressed. It is probable, however, that the majority of men find sexual excitement in a much milder form of voyeurism, limited to observation of their own sex partner or even enjoyment of the pictures in "men's magazines."

vulva The vulva is the external genital area of the female. Included in the vulva are the labia, the clitoris, the mons veneris, and the openings of both the vagina and the urethra.

See also: **clitoris, labia, urethra, vagina**

Wasserman test The Wasserman test is the most commonly used test to diagnose syphilis, one of the venereal diseases. It consists of taking a blood sample and mixing it with chemicals to see if a reaction is produced. If a reaction occurs, the test is positive, and the person probably has syphilis. If no reaction occurs, the test is negative, and the person probably does not have syphilis.

See also: **marriage license, venereal disease**

weaning, see **breast feeding**

wet dream, see **seminal emission**

wife A wife is a woman who has joined in marriage with a man. The word *wife* comes from the old English word *wif* meaning *woman.*

For centuries past, wives were not considered equal to their husbands. They were looked upon as belonging to the husband, and were thought to be incapable of making major decisions in the household. In modern societies ideas have changed, and laws have been passed to make partners in the marriage more nearly equal.

As a wife, a woman joins with her husband in sharing marital responsibilities to establish and maintain a household, to be faithful, to have sexual intercourse, and to give care and guidance to children born of the marriage.

See also: **husband**

withdrawal, see **contraception**

womb, see **uterus**

zygote Zygote is the first of three general terms used to refer to a developing infant. From the time of fertilization until the second week of its growth, the cell mass that develops after the union of egg and sperm is called a *zygote*. From the second week to the eighth week it is an *embryo*, and from the eighth week until birth it is a *fetus*.

See also: **embryo, fertilization, fetus**

INDEX

A

Acne, **1**, 39
Acquired characteristics, *see*
    Characteristics; Environment
Adolescence
    boys' changes during, **1**, 35-49
    description of **1**, 32, 36
    girls' changes during, **1**, 51-69
    how body grows during, **1**, 25-33
    normal growth during, **1**, 91-107
    preparation for marriage, **2**, 129-131
Adolescents, *see* Adolescence
Adoption, **2**, 138-139
Adrenal glands, *see* Endocrine glands
Adults, talking to, **3**, 267-270, 275-279
    See also Husband; Man; Parents;
    Wife; Woman
Afterbirth, **2**, 186-187
Alcohol, **3**, 327
Amnion, **2**, 148-149, 152-157, 180, 182
Androgens
    in males, **1**, 45-47, 56
    in females, **1**, 47
Animals, *see* Life cycle, animal
Appearance, improving, **2**, 218-219
Arguments, **3**, 266, 271-272
Attractiveness, **3**, 283-285, 288-289, 303-304
Automobiles, adolescents in, **3**, 326-328
Average, compared to normal, **1**, 91-93

B

Baby (Babies)
    average birth size, **1**, 92; **2**, 221-223
    a woman's body prepares for, **1**, 59-64
    determination of birth date, **2**, 164-165, 175
    development before birth, **2**, 141-157
    growth of, **2**, 221-233
    heredity of, **2**, 145-146, 211-217
    how life begins for, **1**, 20-21; **2**, 133-135, 141-145
    number born per year, **2**, 236
    sameness of, **1**, 109-110; **2**, 205-207
    See also Birth; Family; Newborn
"Baby blues," **2**, 241
"Baby fat," *see* Weight
Basic food groups, **1**, 72-75

Beards, growth of, **1**, 38, 103
Behavior, individuality in, **1**, 110-127
Belly button, **2**, 186, 192-193
Birth (childbirth)
    and the life cycle, **1**, 9-17; **2**, 139, 235-236, 246-247
    description of, **2**, 173-187
    predicting time of, **2**, 164-165, 175
    See also Baby; Family; Newborn
Birth canal, *see* Vagina
Birth certificate, **2**, 202-203
Birth defects, **2**, 215-217
Blackheads, **1**, 39
Blood
    exchange between mother and fetus, **2**, 148-150, 162-165
    menstrual, *see* Menstruation
    Rh factor in, **2**, 162-164
Body
    proper care of, **1**, 71-89
    size, increase in, **1**, 20-33, 39-41, 58-59, 93-99
    See also Growth; Shape, body
Bottle feeding, **2**, 224, 227
    See also Breast feeding
Boy (Boys)
    becoming a man, **1**, 35-49; **3**, 310-311
    dating for, **3**, 297-307
    girls' telephoning, **3**, 274-275
    growth of, **1**, 25-33, 35-49
    normal development of, **1**, 91-107
    sexual feelings of, **3**, 309-323
    what he likes in a girl, **3**, 283-285
Brain, sleep's effect on, **1**, 86-89
Breech birth, **2**, 183
Breast feeding, **2**, 198-200, 226-227
    See also Bottle feeding
Breasts
    development of, **1**, 57-59, 105
    during pregnancy, **2**, 161, 170
    girls' worries about, **1**, 91, 104-105
    tenderness of, **1**, 57, 68, 105
    See also Breast feeding
Build, body, *see* Shape, body

C

Caesarean section, **2**, 186
Calories, **1**, 75, 78, 81
Cars, adolescents in, **3**, 326-328

485

Castration, **2,** 138
Cell (Cells)
  and heredity, **2,** 208-217
  division of, **1,** 13-15; **2,** 210-211
  description of, **1,** 12-13
  in developing baby, **1,** 15, 20-21; **2,** 141, 145-153, 157
  parts of **1,** 13; **2,** 209
  specialization of, **1,** 20-21, 26-28
Cervix, **1,** 54; **2,** 142, 164, 180, 182
Characteristics
  acquired, **2,** 206-208, 218-219
  inherited, **2,** 206-207, 210-217
Cheating in school, **1,** 122-123
Childbirth, *see* Birth
Children
  brothers, sisters, **2,** 243-245; **3,** 342
  desire to have, **2,** 137-139, 236-239
  growth of, **1,** 25-33; **2,** 221-233
  relations to family, **2,** 232-233, 235-247; **3,** 249-263
  understanding parents, **3,** 255-260, 275-279, 325-332, 334-337
  See also Boy; Family; Girl
Chromosomes
  in fertilization, **2,** 145-146, 211-215
  influence on heredity, **1,** 28; **2,** 209-217
Cigarettes, **3,** 328
Circumcision, **2,** 202
Climacteric, **1,** 62
Clitoris, **1,** 58; **2,** 133-134
Colostrum, **2,** 199
Competition, **2,** 243-245
Compliments, **3,** 269-270
Conception, *see* Fertilization
Condom, description of, **2,** 136
Confidence, **1,** 113-117; **3,** 312-313
Conformity, *see* Social pressure
Contractions, labor, **2,** 178-180, 183-184, 186-187
Contraception, **2,** 135-137, 236
Conversation
  for boys on dates, **3,** 300-301, 304
  for girls on dates, **3,** 282-285
  learning the art of, **3,** 265-272
  telephone, **3,** 272-275
  with adults, **3,** 267-270, 275-279
Cooperation with parents, **3,** 332-337
Courtesy, **3,** 265-266, 300

Cramps, menstrual, **1,** 68-69
Crying instinct, baby's, **2,** 223-224
"Crush"
  step toward real love, **3,** 340, 345-349, 357-359
  reasons for, **3,** 346-347
Cytoplasm, *see* Cell, parts of

D

Dating (Dates)
  age to begin, **3,** 281, 297, 334-335
  attractiveness for, **3,** 283-285, 288-289, 303
  breaking a date, **3,** 302-303, 286
  for boys, **3,** 297-307
  for girls, **3,** 281-295
  goodnight kiss, **3,** 287-288, 301-302, 315
  learning about people, **3,** 295, 304, 307, 356-357, 363-365
  money for, **3,** 287, 299, 304-306
  parents' attitudes about, **3,** 334-337
  parents' rules for, **3,** 281, 292-293, 335-337
  reasons for, **1,** 131; **3,** 313, 356-357
  transportation for, **3,** 282, 299
  See also Double-dating; Going steady; Sexual feelings
Decisions, making, **1,** 112-127; **2,** 218-219
Defects, inherited, **2,** 215-217
Delivery, *see* Birth
DeoxyriboNucleic Acid, **2,** 210-211
Dependence during growth, **1,** 20, 31-33; **2,** 224-227, 233, 249-252
Depression, menstrual, **1,** 67-68
Diaphragm, description of, **1,** 136
Diet
  for gaining weight, **1,** 77-78, 81
  for good health, **1,** 71-76
  for losing weight, **1,** 75-77, 81
  in pregnancy, **2,** 165-167
Digestion, **1,** 26-28
Disagreements, **3,** 266, 271-272
Disease, *see* Venereal disease
Divorce, **3,** 262-263
DNA, **2,** 210-211
Doctor, *see* Medical treatment
Dominant genes, **2,** 213
Double dating, **3,** 282-283, 304-305

Drinking, **3,** 327
Driving, **1,** 120-122; **3,** 326-328
Drugs
   dangers of, **1,** 124-125; **3,** 328-329
   types of, **3,** 329
Ductus deferens, **1,** 43
Dysmenorrhea (menstrual cramps), **1,** 68-69

E

Egg (Eggs) (ovum, s., ova, pl.)
   at time of fertilization, **2,** 142-146
   description of, **1,** 52-53
   if fertilized, **1,** 54, 61; **2,** 134-135, 146-149
   if not fertilized, **1,** 54, 62
   influence on heredity, **2,** 211-217
   number of in ovaries, **1,** 60
   ovulation of, **1,** 53, 60-61
   path after ovulation, **1,** 53-54, 61-62; **2,** 142
   within menstrual cycle, **1,** 52-54, 59-64
   See also Fertilization; Heredity
Ejaculation
   description of, **1,** 43
   during masturbation, **1,** 44-45; **3,** 321-322
   during seminal emission, **1,** 44
   during sexual intercourse, **2,** 134, 142-145
Embryo, **2,** 148, 150-152
   See also Baby, development before birth
Emotions
   in boys, **1,** 36-37, 47-49
   in girls, **1,** 51-52, 69
   See also Love; Maturity, emotional
Endocrine glands (endocrine system)
   description of, **1,** 45, 54, 56
   influence on maturation, **1,** 28-30, 45-47, 54, 56
   See also Androgens; Estrogens; Hormones; Pituitary
Environment
   influence of, **2,** 206-208; **3,** 252-255
   and heredity, **2,** 206-208, 217-219
   See also Heredity
Epididymis, **1,** 43
Episiotomy, **2,** 184-185

Erection
   causes of, **1,** 43-45, 106-107; **2,** 134; **3,** 311, 321-322
   of clitoris, **1,** 58
   purpose in intercourse, **1,** 44; **2,** 134
Erogenous zones, **2,** 133-134; **3,** 319
Estrogens
   in females, **1,** 56
   in males, **1,** 47
   progesterone, **2,** 148
Exercise, importance of, **1,** 81-85, 89
External genitals, **1,** 37-38, 58

F

Fallopian tubes, **1,** 53-54, 61-62
   See also Fertilization
Family
   growing up within, **3,** 249-263
   how baby's birth affects, **2,** 235-247
   See also Children; Marriage; Parents
Father
   child's love of, **3,** 340-343
   determines baby's sex, **2,** 146, 215
   love of newborn, **2,** 203, 242-243
   responsibilities of, **1,** 33; **2,** 243; **3,** 325-326
   See also Husband; Mother; Parents
Fertilization (conception)
   and life cycle, **1,** 20-21, 24-25; **2,** 129, 134-135, 142-145
   after sexual intercourse, **2,** 133-135; 142-145
   heredity determined at, **2,** 145-146, 211-217
Fetus, **2,** 141, 148, 152-157, 176-177
Fontanel, **2,** 183
Food, basic groups of, **1,** 72-75
Fraternal twins, **2,** 147
Friends
   and thinking for yourself, **1,** 112-127
   love of, **3,** 340, 342-343
   talking with, **3,** 265-275

G

Generation gap, **3,** 246, 250-252, 277-279
Genes, **2,** 210-217
Genitals
   external, **1,** 37-38, 58
   internal, *see* Reproductive organs

Gestation period, **2,** 141-157, 175
Girl (Girls)
    becoming a woman, **1,** 51-69; **3,** 311-312
    dating for, **3,** 281-295
    growth of, **1,** 25-33, 51-69
    normal development of, **1,** 91-107
    sexual feelings of, **3,** 309-323
    telephoning boys, **3,** 274-275
    what she likes in a boy, **3,** 300-301
Glue, airplane, *see* Drugs, types of
Going steady, **3,** 293-295, 305-307, 332
Gonads, **1,** 45
    See also Ovaries; Testicles
Gonorrhea, *see* Venereal disease
Grandparents, **2,** 245-246
Growth
    before birth, **1,** 20-21; **2,** 141-157
    differences between boys and girls, **1,** 30, 40, 59
    miracle of, **1,** 19-33
    of babies, **2,** 221-232
    of adolescent boys, **1,** 35-49
    of adolescent girls, **1,** 51-69
    of children, **1,** 25-33; **2,** 232-233
    what is normal in, during adolescence, **1,** 91-107
    See also Maturity

H

Hair, body, **1,** 38, 56, 58, 101-103
Heredity
    and environment, **2,** 206-208, 217-219
    defects of, **2,** 215-217
    how it works, **2,** 208-215
    of sex, **2,** 146, 215
    when determined, **1,** 20-21; **2,** 145-146, 211-215
Height
    boys' increase in, **1,** 41, 93-97
    girls' increase in, **1,** 58-59, 93-97
    of newborn baby, **2,** 194, 221
Heroin, *see* Drugs, types of
Homework, **3,** 335
Homosexuality, **3,** 322
Hormones
    influence on boys' maturing, **1,** 45-47
    influence on girls' maturing, **1,** 54-64
    See also Endocrine glands; Pituitary

Honesty, **1,** 116-117; **3,** 265-266, 269
Husband
    and sexual intercourse, **2,** 129-139
    during wife's pregnancy, **2,** 159-161, 174-176, 179
    how to select, **3,** 363-367
    responsibilities of, **3,** 360-363
    See also Father; Marriage; Wife
Hymen, **1,** 65-66
Hypocrisy and prejudice, **1,** 116
Hysterectomy, **2,** 138

I

Identical twins, **2,** 146, 215
Impotence, **1,** 44
Incubator, **2,** 176, 195
Independence, **1,** 20, 31-33; **3,** 337
    See also Maturity; Responsibility
Individuality
    in decisions, **1,** 110-127
    in growth rates, **1,** 93-107
    showing, **1,** 114-127
    special talent, **1,** 111-112
Infatuation, **3,** 357-360
    See also "Crush"
Infertility, **2,** 137-138
Inherited characteristics, *see* Characteristics; Heredity
Instincts, **2,** 223-224; **3,** 316-317
Intelligence, **2,** 218-219
Intrauterine devices, **2,** 136
Intercourse, *see* Sexual intercourse

J

Jealousy, **2,** 243-245
Jobs, **1,** 33
Jokes, **3,** 270-271

K

Kissing
    in adolescence, **3,** 309, 315-316, 319
    in marriage, **2,** 133-134
    on dates, **3,** 287-288, 301-302
    See also Sexual feelings

L

Labor, in childbirth, **2,** 177-185
Laws, purpose of, **1,** 120-122
Learning, infant, **2,** 221, 223-224, 227-233

License, driver's, **3,** 326
Life
  alternatives in, **1,** 126-127
  beginning of, **1,** 14, 20-21; **2,** 133-135, 141-157
  continued by reproduction, **1,** 9-17
Life cycle
  animal, **1,** 19-25; **2,** 226-227; **3,** 316-318
  examples of, **1,** 9-10, 12-17, 19-25
  human, growth during, **1,** 20-21, 23, 25-33, 35-49, 51-69
  human, how it begins, **2,** 129-135, 139, 142-145
  plant, **1,** 19-24
  See also Growth; Reproduction
Liquor, **3,** 327
Listening, **3,** 265-266
Love
  differs from infatuation, **3,** 345-348, 357-360
  in marriage, **2,** 133-135; **3,** 316-320, 360, 363, 365-367
  leading to marriage, **2,** 130-133; **3,** 348-349, 357-363
  learning to, **3,** 314-315, 339-349
  types of, **2,** 225-228, 241-246; **3,** 251-252, 263, 339-349
LSD, see Drugs, types of

M

Make-up, **3,** 284-285
Mammals, **1,** 24-25; **2,** 225-227
  See also Life cycle, animals
Mammary glands, **2,** 198-200, 226-227
Man
  becoming a, **1,** 32-33, 35-49; **3,** 310
  See also Father; Husband
Marijuana, see Drugs
Marriage
  and children, **2,** 129-139, 235-241
  selecting a partner for, **2,** 130-133; **3,** 348-349, 363-367
  what adolescents should know about, **3,** 351-367
  when people are ready for, **2,** 130-133; **3,** 348-349, 363-367
  See also Family; Love
Master gland, see Pituitary
Maternity clothing, **2,** 170-171

Masturbation, **1,** 44-45; **3,** 321-322
Maturity
  emotional, **1,** 33; **2,** 129-131, 139; **3,** 357-367
  sexual, **1,** 32-33; **2,** 130-131; **3,** 355
  shown by responsibility, **3,** 334-337, 360-363
  social, **1,** 33; **2,** 129-131; **3,** 281, 297, 300, 360-363
Medical treatment
  annual examination, **1,** 89
  during pregnancy, **2,** 162-165, 169
  for acne, **1,** 39
  for abnormal growth, **1,** 92
  for infertility, **2,** 138, 161
  for menstrual problems, **1,** 68
  for reducing diet, **1,** 76
  for venereal disease, **3,** 331-332
Meiosis, **2,** 211
Membrane, cell, see Cell, parts of
Menarche, **1,** 59, 62, 105; **3,** 312
Mendel, Gregor, **2,** 208
Menopause, **1,** 62
Menstrual cycle, **1,** 59-64
Menstruation (menstrual flow, period)
  and menstrual cycle, **1,** 59-64
  beginning of, **1,** 59, 62, 105; **3,** 312
  discomfort during, **1,** 67-69
  end of, **1,** 62
  irregularity of, **1,** 62-63, 105
  lack of during pregnancy, **2,** 148, 161-162
  protection during, **1,** 64-67
  purpose of menstrual lining, **1,** 62, 148
Mitosis, **1,** 13-14; **2,** 210-211
Money
  for dating, **3,** 287, 299, 304-306
  spending of single people, **2,** 131-132; **3,** 361-362
Moral codes, **3,** 320-321
Mother
  child's love of, **3,** 340-342, 349
  during pregnancy, **2,** 159-171
  love of newborn, **2,** 200-203, 241-242, 244, 246-247
  See also Father; Parents; Wife
Movies, ratings of, **3,** 330
Muscles, growth of, **1,** 97-100
  See also Shape, body

489

N

Nationality, prejudice about, **1**, 115
Nature, within life cycles, **1**, 9-17, 19-25; **2**, 129-130, 139; **3**, 316-318
Navel, **2**, 186, 192-193
Necking and sexual feelings, **3**, 309-323
Newborn
    hospital care of, **2**, 189-203
    need to be loved, **2**, 225-227
    See also Baby; Birth; Family
Nipples, see Breast feeding; Breasts
Normal growth, adolescent, **1**, 91-107
Nucleus, see Cell, parts of
Nursing, **2**, 198-200, 226-228
Nocturnal emission, **1**, 44
Nutrition
    how it works, **1**, 26-28
    in adolescence, **1**, 71-81, 89
    in pregnancy, **2**, 165-167

O

Oophorectomy, **2**, 138
Oral contraceptives, **2**, 136-137
Organism, **1**, 12
Orgasm, **2**, 134
Ova, see Egg
Ovaries (female gonads)
    and menstrual cycle, **1**, 59-64
    growth of, **1**, 53, 56
    release of egg (ovulation), **1**, 53-54, 59-61
Ovulation
    egg's progress after, **1**, 53-54, 61-62
    in young girls, **1**, 63-64
    within menstrual cycle, **1**, 59-64
Ovum, see Egg

P

Parathyroids, see Endocrine glands
Parents
    how characteristics are inherited from them, **2**, 211-217
    of growing children, **3**, 249-263
    of new baby, **2**, 235-247
    talking with, **3**, 275-279
    understanding, **3**, 255-260, 275-279
    worries about adolescents, **3**, 325-337
    See also Children; Father; Mother

Party, boy-girl, **3**, 282, 337, 344
Penis
    boys' worries about, **1**, 105-106
    erections of, **1**, 43-44, 106-107; **2**, 133-134; **3**, 311
    growth of, **1**, 37-38
    in sexual intercourse, **1**, 37-38; **2**, 133-134
Period, menstrual, see Menstruation
Personality, **1**, 117; **3**, 283-285, 288-289
Petting and sexual feelings, **3**, 309-323
Pill, the, **2**, 136-137
Pimples, **1**, 39
Pituitary (master gland)
    influence on female sex characteristics, **1**, 29-30, 54-64
    influence on male sex characteristics, **1**, 29-30, 45-47
Placenta, **2**, 148-150, 190-191
Plants, see Life cycle, plant
Posture, **1**, 82, 85; **3**, 285
"Pot," see Drugs
Pregnancy
    baby's development during, **2**, 141-157
    duration of, **2**, 175-176
    husband's reaction to, **2**, 238-239
    mother's condition during, **2**, 159-171
    unwanted, in adolescence, **3**, 326, 330, 332
Prejudice
    about nationality, race, religion, **1**, 115-116, 123
    and social pressure, **1**, 123
    and thinking for oneself, **1**, 115-116
Premarital intercourse, problems of, **3**, 318-321, 330-332
Premenstrual tension, **1**, 67-69
Prenatal development, see Pregnancy
Premature baby, **2**, 169-170, 176, 194-195
Primary sex characteristics
    female, **1**, 53-54
    male, **1**, 41-43
    See also Reproductive organs; Secondary sex characteristics
Procreation, see Reproduction
Progesterone, **2**, 148
Prostate, **1**, 43

Protein, **1**, 26-28, 72-74
Puberty
  description of, **1**, 36, 52-53
  in boys, **1**, 35-49
  in girls, **1**, 51-64
  normal development, **1**, 91-107
  See also Adolescence
Pubic hair, **1**, 38, 58, 102
Puppy love, *see* "Crush"

Q

Questions parents ask about dating, **3**, 336-337

R

Race
  and heredity, **2**, 206, 210
  prejudice, **1**, 115-116, 123
Recessive genes, **2**, 213
Religion, prejudice about, **1**, 123
Reproduction (procreation)
  act of, in humans, **2**, 133-135
  continues life cycles, **1**, 9-17, 19-25
  development of baby, **2**, 146-157
  fertilization, **2**, 142-146
  maturation necessary before, **1**, 35-49, 51-69
  See also Reproduction organs
Reproductive cycle, **1**, 59-64
Reproductive organs, female
  cervix, **1**, 54
  Fallopian tubes, **1**, 53-54
  ovaries, **1**, 53-54
  uterus, **1**, 53-54
  vagina, **1**, 54
  See also Reproductive system; individual organs
Reproductive organs, male
  epididymis, **1**, 43
  penis, **1**, 37-38, 43-44
  prostate, **1**, 43
  scrotum, **1**, 38
  seminal vesicles, **1**, 43
  testicles (testes), **1**, 37-38, 41
  urethra, **1**, 43
  vas deferens (ductus deferens), **1**, 43
  See also Reproductive system; individual organs
Reproductive system, **1**, 37, 41-43, 52-64

Responsibility, adolescent, **3**, 332-337
Rh factor, **2**, 162-164
Rhythm method, **2**, 136
Rules of society, **1**, 120-123
  See also Dating, parents' rules for

S

Sanitary belt, pad, **1**, 64-67
Secondary sex characteristics, **1**, 38-41, 46-47, 56-58
Self-confidence, **1**, 114, 116-117
Seminal emission, **1**, 44
Sex
  drive, description of, **3**, 316-318
  drive, purpose of, **1**, 130; **3**, 316
  education, **3**, 258-259
  glands, *see* Ovaries; Testicles
  hormones, *see* Androgens; Estrogens
  when determined, **2**, 146, 215
  without love, **3**, 319-321, 323
"Sex-linked" defects, inherited, **2**, 217
Sexual development
  in boys, **1**, 35-49, 91-107; **3**, 310-311
  in girls, **1**, 51-69, 91-107; **3**, 311-312
Sexual feelings
  age of beginning, **3**, 309-312, 314-316, 318, 321
  cause of conflict in adolescents, **3**, 309-310, 318-323
  control of, **3**, 317, 319, 321, 323
  differences in boys and girls, **3**, 322-323, 355-357
  purpose of, **2**, 133-137; **3**, 316
Sexual intercourse
  begins new life, **2**, 134-135, 142-145
  contraception, **2**, 136-137
  description of, **2**, 133-135
  function of clitoris in, **1**, 58
  in marriage, **2**, 129-139; **3**, 316-320
  of unmarried people, problems resulting from, **3**, 319-320, 326, 330-332
  orgasm during, **2**, 134
  purposes of, **2**, 133-135; **3**, 316
  stimulation before, **2**, 133-134
  stretching of hymen, **1**, 66
  without fertilization, **2**, 135-139
Shape, body
  changes in, **1**, 91, 97-101, 104-105
  feminine, **1**, 51, 56-58
  masculine, **1**, 35, 39-41

Shyness, **3,** 267
Skin color
   influence of heredity, **2,** 206, 210
   prejudice about, **1,** 115-116, 123
Skin problems, **1,** 39
Smoking, **3,** 328
Social activities, possible problems resulting from, **3,** 326-332
   See also Dating
Social pressure
   affects of, **1,** 118-127
   and prejudice, **1,** 115-116, 123
   giving in to, **1,** 123-126
   useful force in society, **1,** 120-123
Species, continuation of, **1,** 9-17, 22-23
Sperm (spermatozoon)
   at time of fertilization, **2,** 142-146
   description of, **1,** 41
   ejaculation of, **1,** 43-45; **3,** 321-322
   formation of semen, **1,** 43
   influence on heredity, **2,** 211-217
Spouse, see Husband; Wife
Standards of society, **1,** 120
Sterility (infertility), **2,** 137-138
Syphilis, see Venereal disease

T

Talking, see Conversation
Talent, **1,** 111-112; **2,** 218-219
Tampon, **1,** 65-67
Teachers, advice of, **1,** 118
Telephone, **3,** 272-275; **3,** 298, 302-303
Testicles (testes), **1,** 37-38, 41-43, 106
Thyroid, see Endocrine glands
"Trips," LSD, see Drugs, types of
Twins, fraternal, identical, **2,** 146-147

U

Umbilical cord, **2,** 149-150, 155, 186, 190, 192-193
Urethra, **1,** 43, 58
Uterus (womb)
   and menstrual cycle, **1,** 59-64
   changes during pregnancy, **2,** 148-149, 155-157, 166-167, 177
   contractions during childbirth, **2,** 178-180, 183-184, 187
   development of baby in, **2,** 141-157, 159-160, 176-177
   growth of, **1,** 53-54, 56

V

Vagina
   and menstrual cycle, **1,** 59-64
   and hymen, **1,** 65-66
   and sexual intercourse, **2,** 134
   and tampons, **1,** 65-67
   birth canal, **1,** 54; **2,** 164, 180, 183, 185-186
   description of, **1,** 54
   growth of, **1,** 54, 56
Values of society, **1,** 120
Vasectomy, **2,** 138
Vas deferens, **1,** 43
Venereal disease (syphilis, gonorrhea)
   and pregnancy, **2,** 162
   dangers of, **3,** 330-332
   how spread, **3,** 331
Voice change, **1,** 38, 41, 58, 103-104
Vulva, description of, **1,** 58

W

Water, **1,** 75, 78
Weight
   "baby fat," **1,** 40-41, 75-76, 97
   during pregnancy, **2,** 166-167
   gain before menstruation, **1,** 67
   gain during adolescence, **1,** 58-59, 75-76, 97-99
   of newborn baby, **2,** 221-223
   of young child, **2,** 232
"Wet dream," **1,** 44
Wife
   and sexual intercourse, **2,** 129-139
   how to select, **3,** 363-367
   responsibilities of, **3,** 360-363
   See also: Marriage; Mother; Husband
Woman
   becoming a, **1,** 32-33, 51-69; **3,** 311-312
   See also Mother; Wife
Womb, see Uterus
Worries of parents; see Parents

XYZ

X-rays and conception, **2,** 161
Yolk sac, baby's, **2,** 151
Zygote, **2,** 147-148
   See also: Baby, development before birth